PITFALLS OF OBJECT-ORIENTED DEVELOPMENT

BY BRUCE F. WEBSTER

M&T BOOKS

 **M&T Books**
A Division of MIS:Press, Inc.
A Subsidiary of Henry Holt and Company, Inc.
115 West 18th Street
New York, New York 10011

Library of Congress Cataloging-in-Publication Data

```
Webster, Bruce F.
    Pitfalls of object-oriented development : a guide for the wary
and the enthusiastic / Bruce F. Webster
        p.   cm.
    Includes bibliographical references and index.
    ISBN 1-55851-397-3
    1. Object-oriented programming (Computer science) I. Title.
QA76.64.W43  1995
005.1'1--dc20                                          95-3201
                                                        CIP
```

98 97 96 95   4 3 2

Editor-in-Chief: Paul Farrell	**Managing Editor:** Cary Sullivan
Project Editor: Debra Williams Cauley	**Development Editor:** Peggy Watt
Technical Editor: Adele Goldberg	**Copy Editor:** Betsy Hardinger
Production Editor: Anthony Washington	

DEDICATION

To Team Banzai

History is made at night.
Character is what you are in the dark.

TABLE OF CONTENTS

INTRODUCTION 1

How This Book Came to Be 1

The Need for Object-Oriented Development 2

The Need for This Book 3

Who Should Read This Book 4

How This Book is Organized 5

References 6

PART I: A (VERY) BRIEF PRIMER ON OBJECT-ORIENTED DEVELOPMENT 7

Basic Concepts of Software Development 7

Basic Concepts of Object-Oriented Development 9

Objects 10

Abstraction 11

Encapsulation 11

Instantiation 12

Inheritance 13

Specialization 14

Polymorphism 16

Type Checking and Message Binding 17

Composition 18

Containment 19

Association 20

Some Expected Benefits of Object-Oriented Development 21

Faster Development 21

Reuse of Previous Work 21

Modular Architecture 22

Management of Complexity 22

Better Mapping to the Problem Domain 22

Client/Server Applications 23

Compound Documents 23

Some OOD Terminology 24

General Object Terminology 24

Language- and Method-Specific Object Terminology 25

Development and Project Terminology 26

References 27

PART II: PITFALLS OF OBJECT-ORIENTED DEVELOPMENT 29

CHAPTER 1: CONCEPTUAL PITFALLS 31

Pitfall 1.1: Going object-oriented for the wrong reasons. 32

Pitfall 1.2: Thinking objects come for free. 34

Pitfall 1.3: Thinking objects will solve all problems. 36

Pitfall 1.4: Thinking that object technology is mature. 38

Pitfall 1.5: Confusing buzzwords with concepts. 40

Pitfall 1.6: Confusing tools with principles. 42

Pitfall 1.7: Confusing presentation with methodology. 44

Pitfall 1.8: Confusing training with skill. .46

Pitfall 1.9: Confusing prototypes with finished products. 48

Conclusions 50

References 51

CHAPTER 2: POLITICAL PITFALLS 53

Pitfall 2.1: Not educating and enlisting management before the fact. 54

Pitfall 2.2: Underestimating the resistance. 56

Pitfall 2.3: Overselling the technology. 58

Pitfall 2.4: Getting religious about object-oriented development. 60

Pitfall 2.5: Not recognizing the politics of architecture. 62

Pitfall 2.6: Getting on the feature-release treadmill. 64

Pitfall 2.7: Betting the company on objects. 66

Conclusion 68

References 69

CHAPTER 3: MANAGEMENT PITFALLS 71

Pitfall 3.1: Adopting objects without well-defined objectives. 72

Pitfall 3.2: Cramming objects down the developers' throats. 74

Pitfall 3.3: Abandoning good software engineering practices. 76

Pitfall 3.4: Not defining and using an effective methodology. 78

Pitfall 3.5: Attempting too much, too soon, too fast. 80

Pitfall 3.6: Assuming linear development. 82

Pitfall 3.7: Allowing the specification to drift or change without agreement. 84

Pitfall 3.8: Allowing new features to creep (or pour) in. 86

Pitfall 3.9: Mistaking feature prototyping with feature completion. 88

Pitfall 3.10: Misjudging relative costs. 90

Pitfall 3.11: Not identifying and managing risks. 92

Pitfall 3.12: Lying to yourself and others 94

Pitfall 3.13: Using the wrong metrics. 96

Pitfall 3.14: Using the wrong developers. 98

Conclusion 100

References 101

CHAPTER 4: ANALYSIS AND DESIGN PITFALLS 103

Pitfall 4.1: Underestimating the need for analysis and design. 104

Pitfall 4.2: Underestimating the difficulty of analysis and design. 106

Pitfall 4.3: Pouring new wine into old bottles (or vice versa). 108

Pitfall 4.4: Not being aware of your blind spots. 110

Pitfall 4.5: Building a too-general or too-complete solution. 112

Pitfall 4.6: Having the wrong number of architects. 114

Pitfall 4.7: Making things too complex. 116

Pitfall 4.8: Designing by enumeration. 118

Pitfall 4.9: Rearchitecting too often or for the wrong reasons. 120

Pitfall 4.10: Rearchitecting too seldom. 122

Pitfall 4.11: Pleasing the wrong audience. 124

Pitfall 4.12: Forcing a new paradigm on users. 126

Conclusion 128

References 129

CHAPTER 5: ENVIRONMENT, LANGUAGE AND TOOL PITFALLS .131

Pitfall 5.1: Targeting the wrong environment for commercial applications. .132

Pitfall 5.2: Deploying the wrong environment in-house. 134

Pitfall 5.3: Believing manufacturers' claims about object orientation. . . .136

Pitfall 5.4: Using C++. 138

Pitfall 5.5: Not using C++. 140

Pitfall 5.6: Not investing in supporting tools and training. 142

Conclusion 144

References 145

CHAPTER 6: IMPLEMENTATION PITFALLS 147

Pitfall 6.1: Coding too soon. 148

Pitfall 6.2: Assuming that encapsulation obviates design and
implementation standards. 150

Pitfall 6.3: Being fooled by the illusion of rapid progress. 152

Pitfall 6.4: Making too many promises without having enough
     time to keep them. 154

Pitfall 6.5: Leaving the details for later. 156

Pitfall 6.6: Rewriting subsystems in a single bound. 158

Pitfall 6.7: Failing to document and remember key concepts and decisions. 160

Pitfall 6.8: Being seduced by the dark side. 162

Conclusion 164

References 165

CHAPTER 7: CLASS AND OBJECT PITFALLS 167

Pitfall 7.1: Confusing **is-a, has-a,** and is-implemented-using Relationships. 168

Pitfall 7.2: Confusing interface inheritance with
     implementation inheritance. 170

Pitfall 7.3: Using inheritance badly. 172

Pitfall 7.4: Having base classes do too much or too little. 174

Pitfall 7.5: Not preserving base class invariants 176

Pitfall 7.6: Converting non-object code straight into objects. 178

Pitfall 7.7: Letting objects become bloated. 180

Pitfall 7.8: Letting objects ooze. 182

Pitfall 7.9: Creating Swiss Army knife objects. 184

Pitfall 7.10: Creating hyperspaghetti objects and subsystems. 186

Conclusion 188

References 189

CHAPTER 8: CODING PITFALLS 191

Pitfall 8.1: Copying objects. .192

Pitfall 8.2: Testing objects for equality and identity. 194

Pitfall 8.3: Not keeping track of objects. 196

Pitfall 8.4: Consuming memory inadvertently. 198

Pitfall 8.5: Confusing switch statements and polymorphism. 200

Conclusions 202

CHAPTER 9: QUALITY ASSURANCE PITFALLS **203**

Pitfall 9.1: Forgetting the combinatorial explosion. 204

Pitfall 9.2: Neglecting component testing. 206

Pitfall 9.3: Thinking about testing after the fact. 208

Pitfall 9.4: Underestimating testing and support requirements and costs. .210

Conclusion 212

References 213

CHAPTER 10: REUSE PITFALLS **215**

Pitfall 10.1: Underestimating the difficulty of reuse. 216

Pitfall 10.2: Having or setting unrealistic expectations. 218

Pitfall 10.3: Being too focused on code reuse 220

Pitfall 10.4: Not investing in reuse. 222

Pitfall 10.5: Generalizing after the fact. 224

Pitfall 10.6: Allowing too many connections. 226

Pitfall 10.7: Allowing circular dependencies. 228

Conclusion 230

References 231

PART III: MAKING IT WORK **233**

Making a Mid-Course Correction 233

Starting a New OOD Project 236

Afterword 238

References 240

BIBLIOGRAPHY **241**

INDEX **251**

ACKNOWLEDGMENTS

As noted in the introduction, much of this book draws upon my experience since 1990 at Pages Software, Inc. I appreciate all that I have learned from and with Team Banzai: Kevin Berg, Sean Church, Rick Gessner, Debbie Haygood, Bruce Henderson, Nardy Henigan, Greg Kostello, Peter Linss, Carolyn Miller, Mike Parker, Deirdre Poeltler, and Vic Spindler. Special thanks go to Jim Hamerly and Dave Krich, my comrades-in-arms against a sea of troubles, and to Larry Spelhaug, for supporting my writing even when he wasn't entirely sure just what I was going to say.

Beyond that, I have spent time scouring various books and magazines related to object-oriented development for pitfalls beyond those I know from personal experience. I want to make special note of three other collections of object-oriented development pitfalls, two of which use that same term, and all of which I came across after signing the contract and turning in a detailed outline for this book:

Jan Steinman, "The overselling of object technology" in *Object Magazine* 2(3), Sep/Oct 1992.

Adele Goldberg's "Wishful thinking" column in *Object Magazine* 3(2), Jul/Aug 1993.

Taligent, Inc. *Taligent's Guide to Designing Programs*, Reading, Mass.: Addison-Wesley, 1994.

Thanks go to Carole McClendon and Belinda Catalona of the Waterside Agency for promoting my proposal; to Brenda McLaughlin for accepting it; to Peggy Watt for developmental editing; to Betsy Hartinger for copy editing; and to Debra Williams Cauley at M&T Books for working with me to help get this book out the door.

Adele Goldberg's frank, detailed feedback made the book clearer, stronger and more accurate than it would have been otherwise, all the more so because of our disagreements.

My loving and supportive wife, Sandra, and all our kids endured the burden of having me working on two books at once while holding down a full-time job, with a move to a new house thrown in. Looks like my scheduling skills still need work.

As always, all responsibility for the contents of this book is mine.

Bruce F. Webster
San Diego, California
January, 1995

WHY THIS BOOK IS FOR YOU

Object-oriented development (OOD) has been touted as the next great advance in software engineering. It promises to reduce development time, increase code reuse, and provide a competetive edge to companies that use it. While the benefits and advantages of OOD are real, excessive hype has lead to unrealistic expectations among executives and managers, while developers are often miss the subtle but profound differences between OOD and classic software development.

Pitfalls of Object-Oriented Development takes a hard, honest look at the snares and traps awaiting those venturing into this new realm. Based on hard-bought, real-world experience, it can be used by developers, managers, and executives alike to detect and prevent pitfalls, and to take active steps to ensure the success of commercial and in-house OOD projects.

In addition, it can be a valuable guide to small development firms and individual programmers who are using or learning object-oriented languages such as Smalltalk, C++, Object Pascal, and Objective-C for their own development purposes.

This book can also serve as a "real-world" balance for instructors and students in educational settings who are studying object-oriented development. Likewise, it can be a resource to the non-technical readership who have been exposed to OOD through articles in business and news magazines, or who must research and write about these subjects.

FOREWORD

Bruce sent me his manuscript in October of 1994. The issues were familiar; I've seen them in my own and other manuscripts.

In fact, I had just completed the final manuscript for *Succeeding With Objects: Decision Frameworks for Project Management*, a book that captured my and Kenny Rubins's four years of case studies, consulting, discussing, writing, rewriting—all with essentially the same purpose as Bruce's own efforts. Four other manuscripts were on my desk as well. The range of style and content was awesome, although the intended audience for all of the books was the same.

All of the authors are experienced software development managers. All had faced the late schedule, the plan with creeping features, the team that stopped communicating, the quality assurance effort that took the resource hit. All wanted to warn others who would follow as software managers and team members to take care—the extra effort takes time but the payoff comes on the current project and others to follow.

Kenny and I took a very detailed pathway, providing step-by-step processes for setting up projects to transition an organization from where it is to where it wants to be. We express a value-driven approach to planning and executing projects: decide what you want in products, in processes that lead to products, and in resources available to carry out the processes. You should set your expectations for the use of object-oriented technology only after you understand these desires. You determine which of the potential benefits of the technology make sense to pursue. We explore these ideas in processes for developing software; processes for managing corporate-wide reuse programs; and processes for training, selecting development environments, setting up teams, and establishing measurement programs.

Bruce tackles a similar problem but from a different angle. We chose to cast our experience in terms of mottoes—personal battle scars—and anecdotes from our own projects and from case studies. Bruce chose to expose his hard-earned personal scars in the form of pitfalls. This book states the pitfalls, how to recognize them, why they are danger signals, and what to do to get help. Bruce is often very personal in describing his pitfalls, without admitting why. His writing—sometimes sarcastic, sometimes scolding, but always full of conviction—covers the right stuff. When he says: "Worry about this..." then you should worry. Once he has your attention, then you should get to work understanding how to fix your current problems and avoid them in the future. The key is to recognize which hole you dug, and stop digging.

Adele Goldberg
Chairman, ParcPlace Systems

INTRODUCTION

How This Book Came to Be

Somewhere into our third year of the Pages project—developing a full-blown, commercial object-oriented document processor—I was sitting in my office, rereading *The Mythical Man-Month* by Frederick P. Brooks. Dave Krich, our director of quality, wandered by, looked in, and quipped, "Isn't it a little late for that?"

It was indeed. We were approaching our originally announced release date, and we knew we weren't going to make it. But Dave's comment and Brooks' book set me to thinking about all that I wished I had known when I blithely started the Pages development effort some years earlier. I started making a list—mentally at first, and then on paper—of the pits we had fallen into along the way. I added those we had skirted and those we had avoided outright.

This was at the start of 1993. At about that same time, NeXT Computer, Inc. put out a call for session proposals for its NEXTSTEP Developers Conference to be held simultaneously with the NeXTWORLD Expo in May of that year. I sent in a proposal for a session titled "The Pitfalls of Object-Oriented Development." The conference coordinators welcomed the session but were uncomfortable with the title—which was not surprising, given how NeXT had been touting the benefits of OOD. Being more interested in helping others than in proving a point, I changed the title to "Succeeding with Object-Oriented Development," which the conference coordinators found more acceptable. But my materials for the session—which I shared with Jayson Adams, a brilliant developer and chief scientist of Millennium Software—stayed the same, focusing on pitfalls and how to prevent them.

Encouraged by feedback from the session, I worked up a proposal for a book on the same subject. It gave a rough outline and listed a dozen or so sample pitfalls—based on the ones I had used in my presentation, but I indicated that there would be more. Even I didn't realize what an understatement that would be.

The proposal was accepted by M&T Books in fall 1993, and a contract was signed early in 1994. Shortly after that, I sent a more detailed outline with more than 30 pitfalls. As the year went along—and especially as I looked for new pitfalls in other sources—the list grew and grew. The final total: 82 pitfalls are listed in the book you now hold in your hands.

The Need for Object-Oriented Development

Lest anyone misunderstand, I am not an opponent or critic of object-oriented development. On the contrary, I fully believe that it is the most significant development in software engineering since the structured programming revolution of the late 1960s and early 1970s. Indeed, without OOD, I question whether we would be able develop and deliver the complex and reliable software required to keep up with our technological infrastructure.

A case in point: In March 1984, Wayne Holder and I shipped SunDog: Frozen Legacy, a complex, real-time adventure game for the Apple II, which had a 1-MHz, 8-bit 6502 processor. With its graphical user interface using overlapping windows, icons, menus, and joystick-only input, SunDog pretty much pushed the limits of the Apple II. It required 64-KB of RAM and even then swapped segments of code into memory on demand. We used a double-sided floppy disk, giving us 280-KB of disk storage. Code size: 15,000 lines of Pascal and 5,000 lines of 6502 assembly language. I was the principal programmer, writing more than 90 percent of the code; from inception to shipment, the project took 15 months.

Ten years later to the month—March 1994—Pages Software, Inc. shipped Pages by Pages, the document processor mentioned at the start of this introduction. Pages runs under NEXTSTEP 3.0 or later; typical system requirements are a 25-MHz 68040, 33-MHz 80486, or HP-PA RISC system, all 32-bit processors. The application assumes virtual memory (which NEXTSTEP provides), but it is recommended that users have at least 16-MB of memory and 20 MB free on a 300- to 500-MB hard disk drive. Code size: 350,000 lines of Objective-C, which doesn't count all the graphical user interface support provided automatically by NEXTSTEP's class libraries. The engineering team grew to encompass ten people, and the product shipped nearly four years after Pages Software was founded.

Imagine what desktop systems and user expectations and operating system requirements will be like in March 2004. Straight-line extrapolation says we're looking at 500-MHz systems with 1 to 4 gigabytes (GB) of RAM and a 20- to 100-GB hard disk drive. Common sense may make you question those figures—after all, how could anyone ever use up 100 GB of disk space?—but I use 1 GB right now and have a constant need for more space.

Now imagine the software required to make such systems effective and useful. To manage the constant rise in complexity, we need outstanding, effective object-oriented development—and a good deal more, I might add. But by and large, outstanding, effective object-oriented development is what we don't have.

The Need for This Book

I am not a curmudgeon. I struggle daily against the boundless optimism that gets so many developers into trouble and that has certainly landed me in trouble from time to time over the last 20 years. All I have to do to thoroughly embarrass myself—to literally make myself blush—is to drag out my original development schedule predictions from the early days at Pages Software.

But it is exactly that experience that led me to realize how far we as an industry have to go in managing and applying object-oriented development. Talking with other developers and reading in the literature made it clear that my experiences were by no means unique; indeed, many of the pitfalls here are ones that by luck or skill, we managed to avoid but others did not.

Unfortunately, these pitfalls threaten to undermine the acceptance and use of object-oriented development before its promise can be achieved. Precisely because of the hoopla surrounding OOD, expectations are high. Delays and failures, when they come, have a greater negative impact. Given the level of hype (which, thankfully, seems to be dying down), even reasonable successes can have a negative impact, because they fail to live up to unrealistic beliefs as to what the outcome should have been.

A scan of this book's table of contents may have led you to think, "Wait a minute—not all these problems have to do just with object-oriented development." Very true. Many of the pitfalls are general to software development, but they are included here for several reasons. They may have a heightened danger or significance in the context of object-oriented development. They may be commonly believed to be eliminated by OOD, when they are not. Or they may threaten to derail object-oriented development projects in spite of the benefits of OOD.

If there is an overriding theme, it's summed up in Pitfall 4.3: Not knowing what we don't know. This book is designed to help point out things that you might not know about object-oriented development and to do it in a manner calculated to get your attention. The image that comes to mind is of the robot from "Lost In Space," waving its arms and exclaiming, "Warning! Danger, Will Robinson! Oozing objects ahead!"

The purpose of this book is to make object-oriented development more useful, reliable, safe, and successful than it might otherwise be. It is not meant to discourage you or reduce your enthusiasm; rather, it's meant to channel it between and around the pitfalls. To quote ParcPlace Systems Inc. CEO Adele Goldberg: "Only optimists can do complex systems." And complex systems are what we're all going to be doing.

Who Should Read This Book

I wrote this book with three groups in mind:

- developers, those who do the actual architecture and implementation
- technical managers, those who oversee the developers
- upper management, those who run the company and make strategic decisions concerning direction and funding

Some pitfalls apply more to one group than another because of their likelihood to encounter the pitfall and their ability to understand why it's significant. Nevertheless, it's useful—and possibly vital—that all three groups have some degree of familiarity with all the pitfalls listed here. Because this book addresses such a wide-ranging audience, the technical level of the pitfalls varies significantly, starting off low in the first few chapters and gradually getting higher.

Those in upper management have three compelling reasons to understand these pitfalls above and beyond those they may need to avoid themselves. First, they'll find this book a useful reality check on all they may have heard, read, or been told about object-oriented development. Second, they'll be able to better evaluate reports from development groups, understanding the real problems faced by developers and recognizing when they're being fed, ah, horse manure. Third, they'll see that decisions they make—a change in specification, an added feature, a mandate on system configurations—can have a tremendous impact on development schedule or even feasibility, even when the change seems to be a small one.

Technical managers, who form the interface between upper management and developers, will need to watch out for every pitfall in this book. To them I say: You knew the job was dangerous when you took it. I'm probably talking more directly to you throughout this book than to either of the other two groups.

Developers may focus on the more technical pitfalls—those in Chapters 4 through 8—but they need to understand the rest so that they can appreciate the battles that their boss, the technical manager, may have to fight.

By having all three groups familiar with the issues and dangers raised in this book, you can work toward establishing a common understanding and terminology. That will make for better communication, better trust, and better results. This presumes that all three groups want to work toward that end, but if they don't, you have problems even more profound than those addressed in these pages.

How This Book is Organized

Part I, A Brief Primer on Object-Oriented Development, provides an overview of concepts and terminology—with the emphasis on "brief." Entire books have been written about what is covered in a few pages here, so this section is provided for convenience, not completeness or thoroughness.

Part II, Pitfalls of Object-Oriented Development, offers ten chapters on pitfalls organized roughly in chronological sequence of phases: Conceptual, political, managerial, and so on through testing and reuse. Each chapter has three parts: an introduction, a set of pitfalls, and a list of references.

Each pitfall occupies two facing pages, which was a discipline that compelled restraint and brevity in some cases. Each pitfall is introduced with the reasons and causes behind it. Then the following items are detailed for the pitfall:

- Symptoms: your first clues that you may be headed for (or already mired within) this pitfall
- Consequences: what will happen if you don't take action
- Detection: proactive steps to see if you are indeed facing this pitfall
- Extraction: how to get out of it once you've fallen in
- Prevention: how to avoid it in the first place

The lines are sometimes fuzzy among symptoms, consequences, and detection, but that's how life is.

After the pitfall chapters is Part III, Making It Work. This section gives pointers on how to redirect a development effort that is in trouble as well as suggestions for the best way to start and run an OOD project to avoid those problems in the first place. Again, there are many fine books on this subject and more appearing each day, so this is meant to be a guide, not a detailed blueprint. Following that section is a list of resources available: books, magazines, journals, electronic sources, seminars, and organizations.

Each section and subsection is meant to be self-contained, allowing you to browse and skip around at will. The goal is let you get in, find the information you need or want, and get out again. After all, with all those deadlines, you don't have much time to spare, do you?

References

Brooks, Frederick P., Jr. *The Mythical Man-Month*. Reading, MA: Addison-Wesley, 1979.

Goldberg, Adele. "Wishful thinking," *Object Magazine*. Vol. 3, No. 2, Jul/Aug 1993.

Webster, Bruce. "Succeeding with object-oriented development," *Proceedings of the 1993 NEXTSTEP Developers Conference*, NeXT Computer, Inc., 1993.

A (VERY) BRIEF PRIMER ON OBJECT-ORIENTED DEVELOPMENT

We hackers linger by our leading edge
Forgetting what is pending in the cache
Till practice hurtles past us, and we crash.
— *Jeff Duntemann, "The Love Song of J. Random Hacker, 1995"*

It's always useful to agree upon concepts and terminology, especially given the diverse audience for this book. You may be a developer, a technical manager, an MIS director, a vice-president, or a CEO. You are having object-oriented development (OOD) thrown at you, and all you know is that it's a buzzword showing up in the trade press to an annoying extent.

The intent of this chapter is to give you some exposure to and familiarity with the concepts underlying object-oriented development. Because this primer will touch on many subjects—each of which is often covered by entire books (such as those listed in the bibliography at the end of this one)—the explanations are by necessity brief, incomplete, and oversimplified.

The first section offers a quick review of concepts and terminology used in software development. Developers and technical managers can skip this section.

The second section introduces the basic concepts of object-oriented development through a series of simple examples that build upon each other.

The third section talks briefly about the often-cited benefits of object-oriented development, giving an indication of how real they are and what are the associated costs.

The final section goes over some terms used throughout the rest of the book, to be sure we both know what I'm talking about.

Basic Concepts of Software Development

Computers process information using sets of instructions. The physical computer equipment—keyboards, monitors, mice, CPUs, hard disks, cables, and so on—is known collectively as **hardware**. The information—documents, databases, numbers, images—is called **data**.

The instructions and associated data that actually allow the hardware to do something are the **software**. There are various levels of software. At the lowest level are very fundamental sets of instructions, often stored in **read-only memory (ROM)**. For example, most personal computers have a **basic input/output system (BIOS)** which provides a standard set of functions for moving data through the hardware.

At the next level are **operating systems**. An operating system is like the hostess at a party, providing refreshments, bathrooms, entertainment, phones, and an environment in which to interact, all while enforcing limits on the guests' behavior and making decisions on whom to let in the door and whom to invite to leave.

In your computer, the operating system provides resources (memory, disk space, CPU time) and reclaims them when they are no longer needed, provides communication channels to hardware devices (disk drives, I/O ports), allows programs to share data, places limits on what programs can do, decides whether a program can be launched, and can force a program to halt execution. Examples of operating systems include MS-DOS (though this is sometimes disputed), MacOS, Windows, OS/2, UNIX in all its many flavors (SCO UNIX, Solaris, NEXTSTEP), and various mainframe operating systems.

Sitting on top of—or sometimes embedded within — an operating system is the **user interface**. The user interface allows you, the user, to launch programs and utilities, move and delete files, and carry out other system operations. Programs that you execute may work within or build on the operating system's user interface, or they may have their own. User interfaces may be command-line driven (MS-DOS, UNIX shell), text-based (MS-DOS), or graphical (Macintosh, Windows, NEXTSTEP, X/Motif).

Finally, various kinds of software can run and be used via the operating system. **Applications** — word processors, spreadsheets, database programs, graphics programs, and so on — allow you to carry out a task, usually to create, manipulate, and store data. **Utilities** tend to provide additional functionality, either for the system (such as virus detection) or for applications (such as spell checking). **Games** and **educational** software have obvious functions. And **development tools** are used to create yet more software, for commercial, in-house, or personal use.

Sometimes an application environment sits on top of the operating system. It provides a standard **application programming interface (API)** for any applications, hiding the operating system and standardizing the user interface. This allows software to be readily ported to (enabled to run on) several operating systems. Forthcoming examples include the **Common Development Environment (CDE)**, the **Taligent application environment (CommonPoint)**, and **OpenStep**.

Development tools help you to create the instructions and information necessary for a new piece of software. A **program editor** lets you create sets of instructions — functions, methods, modules, libraries, objects, programs — to be executed or converted to a form which can be executed. These instructions, known generically as **code**, are usually written in a given **programming language**: assembly, BASIC, Pascal, C, C++, Smalltalk, Objective-C, Eiffel, Lisp, and so on. An **interpreter** reads instructions written in a given language and executes them. A **compiler** converts instructions written in a given language to either an intermediate form (assembly, p-code) or directly to machine language; that is, instructions understandable by the computer hardware. An **assembler** converts assembly language to machine language.

A **debugger** lets you control the execution of the program you're developing, by stepping or tracing through it and examining values. **Source code management (SCM)** tools help keep track of the different chunks of data (such as text files, objects, or database entries) created using the editor. The SCM tools can track different versions of the same chunk, and help prevent two or more engineers from modifying the same data at the same time. **Source code analysis** tools read through the program files and gather information, such as the names of variables and functions, places where they're referenced, and the length of sections of code. **Computer-aided software engineering (CASE)** tools help manage the various units of code and their relationships, and sometimes automatically generate code for you. **Interface construction** tools help you to create the user interface by generating data or instructions or both, to help implement the interface. **Configuration management** tools help coordinate and track all the names, locations, and versions of data chunks necessary to produce a given version of the software you're creating.

Software development, then, is the art and science of creating any or all the different levels of software described above using any or all the different levels of software described above. And you thought this was simple.

Basic Concepts of Object-Oriented Development

As noted in the preceding section, software consists of instructions and information. The instructions are usually collected into discrete sequences: macros, functions, subroutines, and program bodies. The information is usually collected into discrete chunks: bit streams, variables, strings, and data structures. The instructions usually do something to the information — create it, display it, analyze it, modify it — which is why one of the oldest names for work done using computers is **data processing**.

Each instruction or set of instructions transforms the program from one **state** (condition, set of values) to another. In many cases, the software is designed to respond to a series of **events**, such as user input, arrival of and requests for data, and information about the state of other sets of instructions.

Most approaches to software engineering and development have typically focused on the processing, the data, the states, or the events. But focusing on one of these elements tends to slight the others. That's why objects have caught on: They help to merge the four together. The terminology for object concepts hasn't merged quite as well, so multiple terms may be offered for a given concept.

Objects

You can think of an **object** as an entity that responds to a set of **messages**. A given message causes the object to execute a given set of instructions, known most commonly as a **method** or a **function member**. The object's state is determined by its set of internal data values at any given moment; certain messages can cause its state to change. A message may also represent an event to which the object must respond.

The data values contained by an object are commonly known as **instance variables** or **data members**. Each instance created of a given type of object has its own set of data values.

Messages received by an object tend to fall into several general classes. **Accessor** messages create, set, and retrieve the data in the object. **Action** messages, which inform the object to do something based on its current state and any information passed to it. **Relational** messages define, change, and react to relationships among objects.

Objects were so named because they were first conceived of in terms of writing simulations, which are abstract and limited reflections of the real world. Of course, the vast majority of objects we encounter in the real world are not worth simulating.

For example, I'm sitting at a table, which has a tablecloth on it (courtesy of my wife). Lying on the table (or, more precisely, on the tablecloth) are the following items: my watch; the cap to a hairspray can; a large "thirst buster" mug for holding soft drinks; a round glass paperweight; a large "weather clock" with a large time dial, as well as smaller dials for temperature, barometric pressure, and humidity; a red notebook with an earlier draft of this book; the remote control for the stereo to which I'm listening; a stack of papers, including an old flight itinerary, a "missing books" notice from my son's school, and my daughter's application to a compact disc club; and the monitor, keyboard, mouse, and mouse pad for the computer I'm using to write this book. The room itself is full of air, sound (compression waves carried by the medium of air), electromagnetic waves (light, radio waves, and the occasional stray cosmic ray), and gravity (which may also be a wave).

Abstraction

This list of objects is pretty boring and pointless, right? Right. But it leads us to our first concept of object-oriented development: **abstraction**. Abstraction means distilling the object or objects down to the essence of what you need to represent. For example, if the point of my program is to simulate or monitor the environment, then the only object in my room that I'm actually interested in is the weather clock. Furthermore, I don't want or need to represent how big it is, how it is shaped, or what color it is; those aren't relevant to the scope of my program. Instead, I just care that I can use it to get the current time, temperature, barometric pressure, and humidity. The result is the appropriate abstraction for my program. If I were instead dealing with stresses on the tabletop, then my clock abstraction would focus on size, shape, orientation, and center of gravity, and the various readouts would be irrelevant.

WeatherClock	
Time	Barometric Pressure
Temperature	Humidity

Figure P.1 WeatherClock is an abstraction of an actual clock. It encapsulates (hides) its workings and can be used via a set of messages (methods).

Encapsulation

Looking at the weather clock, I see four dials, which give me the current values for time, temperature, barometric pressure, and humidity. These dials form the clock's **interface**. I don't see the clockwork, thermometer, barometer, and humidity gauge which calculate or measure the appropriate information and update the dials. These items all make up the clock's **implementation**, which is hidden inside the clock. This is the second concept of OOD: **encapsulation**. An object encapsulates, or contains, its implementation; all it shows to the outside world is its interface.

The interface determines what information and actions can be requested of the object; the implementation determines how those requests are actually carried out. In theory, for example, I could replace the barometic mechanism in my weather clock for a different one. The clock's interface wouldn't change — I wouldn't have to go around giving everyone new instructions on how to read the barometric dial — but the barometer's implementation would have changed.

Instantiation

Now suppose I have a second weather clock in the room, over on the far wall. Both clocks have identical interfaces and identical implementations, but their current information may differ; the timekeeping portions may not be in sync, and there may be differences in the temperature and humidity readings, because one is close to an open window. To represent the two clocks in my program, I need two sets of data, but a single interface and implementation of instructions.

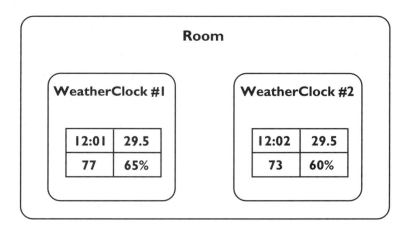

Figure P.2 Two instances of the WeatherClock object class, each with its own separate data values.

This leads us to the third concept of OOD: **instantiation**. First, I define a general WeatherClock class. This class declares the appropriate WeatherClock interface, defines the WeatherClock implementation (using instructions), and specifies the information (data) that each separate weather clock maintains. I can now **instantiate** — create an instance of — each WeatherClock object that I need. I can have two, 20, or 2,000 WeatherClock objects, each with its separate set of data.

Regardless of how many WeatherClock object instances I create, I have only one WeatherClock class, which contains the instructions that operate on that data. I need only one set of instructions, since they are the same for each and every WeatherClock object. This not only saves space, but also guarantees that each and every WeatherClock behaves the same given the same set of data.

Inheritance

As you may remember, there was also a watch on the table. If I wanted to create a DigitalWatch object, I would abstract out the relevant aspects — say, time, date, and event alarms, which go off at a given time on a given date — and create the appropriate class. I might then note that DigitalWatch and WeatherClock have identical central information and functionality: updating and making available the current time. In other words, they are both timepieces — a more general classification. I could simply duplicate the WeatherClock's "timepiece" code and data specification in the DigitalWatch class. However, that would lead to the risk of fixing a bug or improving functionality in one class, and then forgetting to do the same for the other class. And if I had an alarm clock, a pocket watch, and several other timepieces, that risk — and the corresponding effort required to make sure all classes behaved the same — would be much greater.

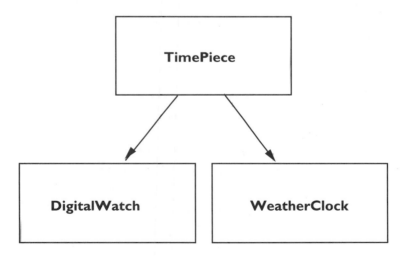

Figure P.4 DigitalWatch and WeatherClock are subclasses of TimePiece, which means that they inherit TimePiece's methods and instance variables.

The solution lies in the fourth concept of OOD: **inheritance**. I create a TimePiece class, which specifies the data required for all timepieces, declares the standard time-piece interface—get current time, set current time, and so on —and defines the implementation (instructions that manipulate or access the data to carry out the operations listed in the interface). TimePiece is my **base class** or **superclass**. I now declare the DigitalWatch and WeatherClock classes to be **derived classes**, or **subclasses**, of TimePiece. By so doing, I ensure that they inherit TimePiece's interface, implementation, and data specification. This allows me to reuse code for multiple classes, just as the notion of a class allowed me to reuse code for multiple object instances. And the same benefits apply: Any changes I make to TimePiece are automatically inherited by all its subclasses and thus by all the instances of each subclass.

Some object-oriented programming languages (OOPLs), most notably C++, allow you to separate **interface inheritance** and **implementation inheritance.** You can inherit the interface but no implementation; you can inherit the implementation, but no inter-face; or you can inherit both. These alternatives affect the relationship between the superclass and its subclass. For more details on what this means and some of the related pitfalls, see Chapter 7 ("Class and Object Pitfalls").

Some OOPLs (including, again, C++) support **multiple inheritance**. This means that a given class can have two or more superclasses, inheriting data, interface, and implementation from all of them. As you can imagine, this has some pitfalls all its own; however, they tend to be language-specific, and so I defer them to the appropriate books (for example, see the C++ books listed in the Bibliography). Many programmers argue whether the benefits of multiple inheritance outweigh the dangers, but it's a standard feature of the most predominant OOPL, so that's a moot point. The most benign use is probably implementing polymorphism (see below), but use it cautiously anyway.

Specialization

It's clear from the description above that DigitalWatch and WeatherClock are not iden-tical classes; yet if all I do is declare them subclasses of TimePiece, that's how they'll behave. Thus the fifth concept of OOD: **specialization**. I need to specialize each class, that is, to add the data specification, interface, and implementation details that will dis-tinguish it from TimePiece. Based on the description above, DigitalWatch needs to be extended to keep track of the current date and to support time/date alarms. Likewise, WeatherClock needs to have the temperature, barometric pressure, and humidity func-tions added. The relationship between TimePiece and its two subclasses is known as the **is-a** relationship: a DigitalWatch (or WeatherClock) **is-a** TimePiece, while the reverse (TimePiece **is-a** DigitalWatch) is not true.

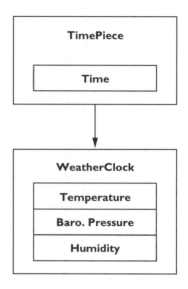

Figure P.4 WeatherClock is a specialization of a TimePiece, inheriting its Time implementation and adding some new ones of its own.

There are three general types of specialization. The first occurs by adding new information and methods. This is shown above, where both DigitalWatch and WeatherClock add new data and functionality to that declared in TimePiece.

The second type of specialization is replacing (**overriding**) inherited data and methods with your own. For example, the TimePiece class data and implementation might assume time precision to one second. DigitalWatch, on the other hand, might keep accuracy to 0.01 second. It would then replace the TimePiece implementation with its own; it might also extend the interface to allow the current time to be set or retrieved with values to 0.01 second.

The third type of specialization is blocking inherited functionality, either by removing part of the inherited interface or replacing part of the inherited implementation with an implementation that does nothing. A somewhat contrived example is a SealedClock class, a subclass of TimePiece, whose current time can be read but (after initialization) cannot be set. Although there are valid reasons for doing this, recognize that it may lead you into one or both of the first two pitfalls in Chapter 7.

Polymorphism

The sixth concept of OOD is **polymorphism**. The meaning of the term isn't obvious from its Greek roots, which mean "having many forms." The concept refers to the fact that in OOD, you can have different classes of object that respond to the same method(s). For example, our DigitalWatch and WeatherClock objects both respond to the commands to get and set the current time.

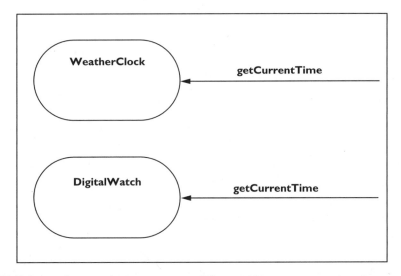

Figure P.5 Polomorphism is when two or more different objects can respond to the same message.

There are three ways of enforcing polymorphism. The first (and strongest) is by interface inheritance. For example, all subclasses of TimePiece can inherit its interface; therefore, unless they choose to block or hide that inheritance somehow, they'll all respond to the commands declared in TimePiece. This approach, however, requires that all such polymorphic classes descend from the same superclass.

The second means of enforcing polymorphism is by protocols. A **protocol** is an interface that can be implemented by various classes; knowing which protocols a given class supports lets you know which commands it can respond to. Different languages have different ways to implement protocols. In C++, you still have to use interface inheritance, but you do it by defining the protocol as a mixin class and then using multiple inheritance. (Note that this is full inheritance, so you also get any data specification and implementation.) In Objective-C, you can actually declare a protocol — which consists only of an interface — and then list in the class interface the protocols it supports. Failure to implement the protocol completely in that class results in compiler warnings.

The third means of enforcing polymorphism is by hand: You just make sure the same method(s) are declared and defined in all the relevant classes. This is relevant only for classes that do not share a common superclass where the method(s) can be declared. The challenge with this approach is the same one mentioned in the section on inheritance: It's hard to ensure consistency and uniformity, especially if you have to change the protocol.

Type Checking and Message Binding

A brief digression is required here. Polymorphism raises the issue of whether an object responds to a given message being sent to it. This is especially true if you have a pointer to an object, because there is no inherent guarantee as to what kind of object is being pointed at. There are two strongly related issues here: type checking and message binding.

Type checking deals with the point at which the type (identity, class) of an object instance is known. **Static** (or **strong**) **type checking** requires that the class (or superclass) of a given object be known when the program is compiled. In **dynamic** (or **weak**) type checking, the type of a given object need not be known until the point at which it becomes relevant during execution. This capability is often associated with a generic object pointer type, such as the **id** data type in Objective-C.

In **static binding** (also known as **early** or **compile-time** binding), the compiler must know at the time of compilation which method will actually get called when a given message is sent to a given object. Static binding helps both with execution efficiency and with reliability.

In **dynamic binding** (also known as **late** or **run time** binding), the compiler doesn't know which method will be called when a given object is being sent a given message; all that will be resolved when the program is executed. Each time the message is to be sent, the run-time system of the language looks behind the curtain to see whether the object can respond to that message. This is known as **message dispatching** and requires additional processing each time the look-up occurs.

C++ requires static binding, though it relaxes this just a bit. You can declare a pointer to a given base class, and then have that pointer actually point to an object belonging to any derived class of that base class. If you have declared the method being called as a virtual function in the base class and in any intervening derived classes, then sending that message to the actual object will cause its implementation of the method to be called. As noted, things were relaxed only a bit.

With dynamic binding, run-time methods often allow you to interrogate an object as to which class it belongs to, whether it descends from a particular class, whether it supports a given protocol, and whether it responds to a particular method call. Nothing comes free; the cost of this flexibility is time (cycles spent looking up to see whether the object does respond to the method) and space (extra overhead in each class and instance to maintain information). Naysayers will hyperventilate about the dangers of weak type checking, ignoring that OOPLs that offer dynamic binding often offer both static binding and run time type checking, allowing you to do all the strong type checking you wish to.

Composition

Back to the subject at hand. We've defined the WeatherClock class as a subclass of TimePiece with specializations to implement the three weather instruments. You may have assumed that these were simply additional methods and data structures added to the class. But suppose there's also a barometer on the wall and a thermometer mounted outside the window. This suggests we may want to define classes for Barometer, Thermometer, and HumidityGauge, all of which might be subclasses of a general class, WeatherGauge. The WeatherClock would then be implemented by pointing to instances of each of those three classes.

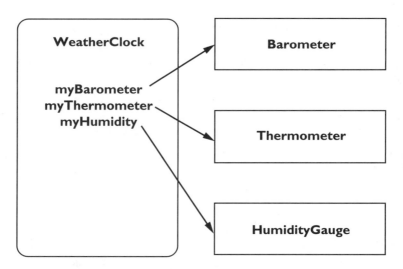

Figure P.6 The WeatherClock object has instance variables that point at three other objects that it comprises.

This is the seventh concept of OOD: **composition**. An instance of WeatherClock contains or is composed of instances of Barometer, Thermometer, and HumidityGauge. This is known as the **has-a** relationship: the WeatherClock instance **has-a** Barometer instance. As with inheritance, this relationship is directional: It is not true that the Barometer instance **has-a** WeatherClock instance.

The **has-a** relationship carries with it a strong notion of ownership: the WeatherClock object owns the Barometer object it comprises. This, in turn, has practical implications, because it can help you decide who has the responsibility to create the Barometer instance in the first place, and to delete or free it when the WeatherClock instance is deleted or freed. The owning object generally has that responsibility, though it may delegate that task to other objects.

Containment

Now suppose that we decide to define and create a Table object to represent what the WeatherClock and DigitalWatch are sitting on. We set up Table to maintain a collection, which is called a **container list**, of all the objects on it. If we model the system here in this room, an instance of Table will be created, and its container list will point to the relevant instances of WeatherClock and DigitalWatch.

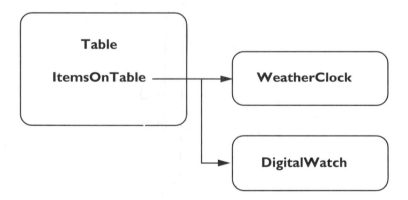

Figure P.7 The Table object has a list that points to all the objects which are "on" the table.

This defines the eighth concept of OOD: **containment**, also known as the **holds-a** relationship. As with **is-a** and **has-a**, **holds-a** is directional: The Table object **holds-a** WeatherClock, but the reverse is not true. There is no sense of ownership: The Table object is not responsible for creating or deleting the WeatherClock object, and the Table object can itself be created or deleted without necessarily affecting the WeatherClock object. Also note that the WeatherClock object can come and go in the Table's collection without affecting the nature, function, or interface of the Table; indeed, the Table could contain several instances of WeatherClock or none at all. Note how this differs from the composition relationship between WeatherClock and Barometer.

Association

Throughout this discussion, we've talked about thermometers, barometers, and humidity gauges without considering how or where they get their values. The implication is that either these instruments interrogate some other object(s) for that data, or some other object(s) notify these instruments that they need to update themselves. In either case, there is a relationship of some duration between two (or more) object instances that is neither inheritance (**is-a**), composition (**has-a**), nor containment (**holds-a**). This is the ninth concept of OOD—**association**—which is the most general of object relationships, **knows-about**. If object A **knows-about** object B, then A has the capability to call any of the methods in B's public interface, but no other relationship beyond that is implied.

Suppose that we define a Person class, instantiate a Person object, and place it in a Room object. The Person object could use appropriate methods to examine the Room's contents and come to know about the Table object; Likewise, it might be able to interrogate the Table and learn about the DigitalWatch and the WeatherClock. The Person can now use the appropriate methods to read the current time from the two timepieces; it may use the time read from one to set the time on the other, synchronizing both.

There are two general types of **knows-about** relationships. One is of temporary duration, usually to accomplish a specific task. A reference to an object is found or retrieved, the desired actions are carried out, and the object is forgotten. The example above of the Person reading the DigitalWatch and the WeatherClock may well be done this way; it is unlikely that the Person object will have explicit data fields for maintaining pointers to either object.

The other type of relationship is of more lasting duration, either to maintain relationships that cannot be reestablished or to save overhead when looking for something. For example, our simulation may define an Atmosphere object to model atmospheric conditions. The WeatherGauge class may then have a data field to point to the appropriate instance of Atmosphere so that any of the weather gauge subclasses — Thermometer, Barometer, HumidityGauge — can get the information it needs to update itself.

This has been a very brief introduction to the concepts of object-oriented development: abstraction (problem refinement), encapsulation (hiding implementation), instantiation (creating objects from classes), inheritance (**is-a**), specialization (subclasses), polymorphism (identical methods), composition (**has-a**), containment (**holds-a**), and association (**knows-about**).

Some Expected Benefits of Object-Oriented Development

Many benefits are cited for object-oriented development, often to a degree that is unrealistic. This section will briefly review the claims and discuss the real benefits. As you read about them, recognize the investments required to achieve each benefit.

Faster Development

Object-oriented development was long touted as leading to faster development, particularly by NeXT in promoting NEXTSTEP for development of mission-critical custom applications (MCCAs). Many of NeXT's claims of reduced development time are correct in principle, if a bit overstated; but these reductions tend to result from several factors: NEXTSTEP's Application Kit, an extensive object class library that aids greatly in user-interface programming; NEXTSTEP's Interface Builder, which aids greatly in user-interface layout and modification and which directly supports object architecture; Objective-C, which is much easier to learn and use than C++; and the fact that most MCCAs have a relatively simple architecture, usually acting as a database front end.

These same benefits don't necessarily exist for all other projects using OOD. Writing a large productivity application for Windows 95 in C++ with OLE 2.0 support is not the same thing as developing a database browser under NEXTSTEP. For that matter, writing a large productivity application under NEXTSTEP is not the same as writing a database browser under NEXTSTEP. To gain all the benefits of OOD, sufficient design and research time must be spent up front; yet that is seldom allowed, because OOD is often adopted to shorten development time.

The real benefit of faster development comes with ensuing projects — either revisions to a given project or creation of new projects that can reuse software from existing ones.

Reuse of Previous Work

Reuse is the benefit cited most commonly in the press, particularly in business magazines. Object-oriented development will produce software modules that will just plug into one another, allowing us to create programs as if we were assembling Tinker Toys.

Leaving aside the specter of living in a house built of Tinker Toys, the analogy is wrong and tends to mislead developers new to OOD. Most OOD software reuse comes from creating general base classes and deriving new classes from them for successive projects. As the base classes gain in functionality and quality, the need to subclass is reduced.

Beyond that, reuse is just plain hard, as discussed in Chapter 10 ("Reuse Pitfalls").

Modular Architecture

Object-oriented systems have a natural structure for modular design: objects, subsystems, frameworks, and so on. But nothing in OOD compels or requires that the code produced will be modular. As much thoughtful care in design and implementation is required to produce a modular architecture in OOD as it is for any other form of software development.

Management of Complexity

Edsger Djikstra, in his classic paper "Programming considered as a human activity," established quietly yet forcefully that software systems beyond a certain size are too complex to be entirely comprehended by a single human being. Most software engineering for the past thirty years has been aimed at reducing and managing complexity, and object-oriented design is no different.

Except that it is different, and not always for the better. Both procedural and data analysis managed complexity by taking a given approach to the problem and successively decomposing it into units that could be comprehended. Mispracticed, object-oriented development often leads to a seething mass of object instances, all talking to each other in ways that are hard to understand, follow, and predict. Principles and practices exist for using object architecture to manage complexity well, but — as with traditional software engineering — they require time, education, and practice. Complexity management does not come for free.

Better Mapping to the Problem Domain

This is a clear winner for object-oriented development, particularly when the project maps to the real world. Whether objects represent customers, machinery, banks, sensors, aircraft wings, or pieces of paper, they can provide a clean, self-contained implementation which fits naturally into human thought processes. Again, this benefit accrues provided those doing the analysis and design are knowledgeable and skilled.

Client/Server Applications

This benefit is another clear winner for object-oriented development. By their very nature, client/server applications involve sending messages back and forth over a network, and the object-message metaphor of OOD meshes nicely with that.

Compound Documents

The current trend toward compound document architectures (OLE 2.0, OpenDoc, Taligent) center on an object or object-like implementation. That's not surprising, given the **has-a** and **holds-a** relationships fundamental to object design.

In short, object-oriented development offers significant benefits in many problem domains, but those benefits must be considered realistically, as must the costs of OOD. The purpose of this book is to help you reduce those costs and maximize the benefits by understanding and avoiding the pitfalls of object-oriented development.

Some OOD Terminology

Many terms have been defined in this chapter, but this section is included to make sure that all the bases are covered. Unfortunately, many different terms are used for the same concept, depending on the language or methodology being used.

General Object Terminology	
object	Generally speaking, an entity combining behavior with relevant attributes and states. In terms of software, a collection of data with the relevant instructions to do something with or to that data.
class	The general declaration and definition of a collection of identical objects. The class specifies the data required for a given instance of itself; it presents the interface, giving the list of available operations; and it contains the implementation of those operations.
message	A command to an object.
instance	An actual copy of an object, with memory allocated for the data specified by the class. A class is instantiated to create an instance.
abstraction	Focusing on what needs to be represented and eliminating what doesn't.
encapsulation	Hiding the details of the object's implementation.
inheritance	Having one class inherit instance variables, methods, interface, and/or implementation from another class.
specialization	When a new object class is a refinement of an existing one; defines the **is-a** relationship.
polymorphism	Having two or more different classes of objects respond to the same message.
type checking	Determining which class an object belongs to. **Strong** or **static** type checking is done at compile time; **weak,** or **dynamic,** type checking is done at run time.
composition	Having an object be built out of other objects; defines the **has-a** relationship.
containment	Having an object be a container for other objects; defines the **holds-a** relationship.
association	One object being able to refer to another; may be bidirectional; defines the **knows-about** relationship.

Language- and Method-Specific Object Terminology

data member	A data field within an object.
instance variable	A data field within an object.
function member	An operation specified within a class.
method	An operation specified within a class.
Class (or factory) method	A method that operates upon a class. Most often used to create an instance or to ask a class for information about itself.
instance method	A method that operates upon an instance.
interface	The set of methods for a given class that is visible to other classes.
implementation	The actual code used to implement the methods for a given class, as well as the defined set of instance variables.
base class	A class from which other classes are derived.
superclass	A class from which other classes are derived.
derived class	A class that is derived from another (base) class.
subclass	A class that is derived from another (super) class.
abstract class	A base class that is never instantiated.
concrete class	A class that is instantiated.
subsystem	A general term for a set of objects that interact with one another.
framework	A collection of related objects that work together to provide a certain class of functionality.
domain	A general term for a given area of functionality or a given problem area.
component	A unit of software designed to integrate and work with other units of software.
program	A unit of software capable of being used on its own.
project	A general term for any software being developed for a given end.

Development and Project Terminology

prototype	A preliminary version of a project developed to demonstrate its interface and planned functionality.
user interface	The presentation a given program makes to a user, along with the controls and commands the user invokes to control the functioning of the program.
analysis	The act of evaluating the problem to be solved and identifying the nature and approach of the solution.
design	The act of evaluating the analysis of a problem and constructing the architecture of the solution.
testing	The act of verifying that the implementation is free from unacceptable errors, correctly reflects the design, and correctly solves the original problem.
development	Analysis, design, implementation, and testing.
paradigm	A particular approach or concept, used especially in software to refer to the way a given task is presented to and handled by the user.
milestone	A significant point in development used to measure or indicate progress in the schedule.
engineer	Refers to someone writing actual code that implements a given design.
architect	Refers to someone performing analysis and design.
developer	Anyone significantly involved in software development: architects, engineers, testers.
technical manager	Someone with schedule and team management responsibilities, and who is responsible for a group of developers.
upper management	Company leaders and managers (usually nontechnical) with authoriy over technical managers.
customer	The person or people for whom the project is being developed. Customers can be other engineers, workers within the company, another company or agency, or commercial users.
software engineering	The set of practices intended to make schedules predictable and to make software correct and reliable.

References

Booch, Grady. *Object-Oriented Analysis and Design with Applications, (2nd ed.)*. Redwood City, CA: Benjamin/Cummings, 1994. (This is for serious developers and real technical managers only. One of the best single-volume introductions to all the major topics and issues in object-oriented development).

Coad, Peter and Edward Yourdon. *Object-Oriented Analysis (2nd ed.)*. Englewood Cliffs, NJ: Yourdon Press, 1991. (Lighter in tone and weight than Booch; very nuts-and-bolts, how-to-do-it).

Djikstra, Edsger. "Programming considered as a human activity," *Proceedings of the 1965 IFIP Congress*, North-Holland Publishing Co., Amsterdam, The Netherlands, 1965.

Taylor, David A. *Object-Oriented Technology: A Manager's Guide*. Reading, MA: Addison-Wesley, 1990. (An excellent, accessible introduction into the concepts of object technology. Of use for both technical and non-technical readers).

PART II:

PITFALLS OF OBJECT-ORIENTED DEVELOPMENT

And finally, I cannot tell you all the things whereby ye may commit sin; for there are divers ways and means, even so many that I cannot number them.

— Mosiah 4:29, *The Book of Mormon*

CHAPTER 1:
CONCEPTUAL PITFALLS...31

CHAPTER 2:
POLITICAL PITFALLS 53

CHAPTER 3:
MANAGEMENT PITFALLS 71

CHAPTER 4:
ANALYSIS AND DESIGN PITFALLS..103

CHAPTER 5:
ENVIRONMENT, LANGUAGE AND TOOL PITFALLS 131

CHAPTER 6:
IMPLEMENTATION PITFALLS..147

CHAPTER 7:
CLASS AND OBJECT PITFALLS 167

CHAPTER 8:
CODING PITFALLS...191

CHAPTER 9:
QUALITY ASSURANCE PITFALLS..203

CHAPTER 10:
REUSE PITFALLS 215

CHAPTER I:
CONCEPTUAL PITFALLS

A little learning is a dang'rous thing;
Drink deep, or taste not the Pierian spring:
There shallow draughts intoxicate the brain,
And drinking largely sobers us again.

—Alexander Pope, An Essay On Criticism

The most general pitfalls have one thing in common: confusion about what object-oriented development (OOD) is and what it entails. There are several reasons this happens.

First, we may get some education, but not enough. Reading articles on OOD, or even a book or two, may create a false sense of confidence and understanding, especially given the "Aha!" rush of insight that often follows. The result is often a blithe walk right into the many pitfalls found in this book, as I know from experience.

Second, we may confuse form with substance. When structured development became the rage in the 1970s, some developers and managers thought that structured development simply meant eliminating GOTO statements and using lots of subroutines. These steps helped, but they were just two surface manifestations of deeper and more significant principles. Similarly, some developers and managers today think that object-oriented development simply means defining classes and creating objects.

Third, we may not recognize all the implications of object-oriented development. A different approach to architecture, design, and coding may require—or, at least, may work best with—different management and scheduling techniques. Attempts to pound a square peg into a round hole may take longer, may jam the peg, and may even crack the board.

Fourth, we may be tempted to abandon or neglect traditional design and software engineering practices. OOD is often adopted because of its promise of increased productivity and shortened schedules, so time is frequently not allotted to make sure that things are done right. However, as a friend of mine used to say, "Life is like the IRS: You can pay now, or you can pay later with interest and penalties."

In all four of these areas, time spent up front will save time later. But that has always been hard to sell to upper management.

Pitfall 1.1: Going object-oriented for the wrong reasons.

There are several valid reasons to move to object-oriented development; they were listed in Part I. Unfortunately, there are many more misunderstood, misguided, or just downright bad reasons for going object-oriented. They include (but are not limited to) the following:

- You (or your boss or your developers) read an article about it.
- You want to cut back on the development staff.
- You think it will eliminate (or significantly reduce) the need for testing.
- You have to complete a project by a certain date.
- You want to complete the project before the currently scheduled date.
- You think you can complete your project five to ten times faster using OOD.
- You think it will eliminate all your software engineering problems.
- You think it will reduce project risk.
- You want to write a program with a graphical interface.
- Someone wants to sell you development tools or a particular application environment.
- You want to be able to build future products by simply plugging software components together.

...and so on.

Symptoms   The other conceptual pitfalls in this chapter are a good first set of symptoms.

Consequences Possible project schedule slip. Failure to achieve expected benefits, resulting in disappointment for yourself and (worse yet) your superiors. Projects become unacceptably late or even fail. Heads roll, including possibly your own .

Detection   Ask all people involved in the decision to use object technology to write down their reasons (in detail) for doing so, along with all the corresponding risks they see. If the answers to the first question match the list above or any of the other pitfalls in this chapter, you're in trouble. If no significant risks are listed, you're in even more trouble.

Extraction   Gather all the key managers and decision makers. Discuss the findings gathered under **Detection**. Explain (carefully) the problems that underlie any faulty reasons. Establish what should be the proper reasons for going object-oriented and what the likely benefits of doing so will be. Reset expectations to the best of your ability.

Prevention   Pretty much the same process as **Detection** and **Extraction**, but do it before you start the process of adoption of object technology. Emphasize very heavily the fact that most benefits of object technology are long term and require significant up-front investment in training, tools, analysis, design, and personnel.

Pitfall 1.2: Thinking objects come for free.

Suppose you were managing a boxer and wanted him to compete in professional karate tournaments. Suppose you gave him some books on karate to study, showed him a film or two, maybe let him attend a three- or four-day karate training session, and then signed him up for a professional karate competition. The chances are that he'd lose, and badly, no matter how good a boxer he was or how earnestly he studied those books.

It sounds silly, doesn't it? Guess what: This scenario has been played out many times in software development groups across the nation and the world. Software developers with no OOD experience—and sometimes with little software engineering training—are given a few books on object-oriented development, are shown some sample OO programs, and may even be sent to a three- or four-day seminar on OOD, C++ programming, or whatever. They are then assigned to a critical development project that is supposed to be completed in record time and to provide code that can be reused for other projects. The results are usually about the same as those for the under-prepared boxer in the karate tournament—if not worse.

Symptoms Reluctance on the part of upper or technical management to devote resources to converting to OOD. A key phrase is, "But I thought that objects were supposed to save money and time, not cost more!" Also—even more dangerously—developers who feel that they have no need of additional OOD training.

Consequences Projects that fail to show significant benefits of object-oriented development: shortened development time, better management of complexity, greater code reuse, and superior mapping of the program solution to the original project.

Detection Ask yourself, "If our developers were going to compete against a group of expert object-oriented developers, how would I have to prepare them?" Your answers should be very illuminating.

Extraction First, raise everyone's awareness of the need to better prepare everyone for OOD. Second, recognize that you're in the middle of a project and there are probably significant deadline pressures, so how much you'll be able to do may be limited. Third, point out that it may well take longer to complete the project without additional investment in objects than it will with that investment.

Prevention   As soon as your company, division, or group decides to go with object-oriented development, ask yourself the question given above in **Detection**. Approach it literally from that angle. As you do, you'll find that there are five key resources that you must invest in:

- **People.** Recruit developers and managers (from inside or outside the company) with significant OOD experience. Budgetary and political constraints may limit what you can do. Also, identify those within your group who are most likely to adapt well to OOD.

- **Time.** It will take time to create good object-oriented architects and developers. Some will learn faster than others, but (to extend the analogy) even the best boxer will have to study and train over an extended period of time to compete well in karate tournaments.

- **Education.** First and foremost, create a cult of learning. Make it clear to developers and technical managers that those who learn the most and apply it will be rewarded. Then start to build the resources. Acquire a large selection of books on object-oriented development and require the appropriate people to set aside time to study them. Subscribe to the relevant journals and magazines. Send people to seminars, trade shows, and other training. Encourage in-house discussions and debriefings on various OOD issues and topics.

- **Tools.** Buy the right tools for the job: editors, compilers, debuggers, and OO-specific tools, such as those for OO analysis and design. Attempts to save money here are almost always misguided and counterproductive; make sure that the tools are worthwhile, but if they are, buy them and train the developers on them.

- **Practice.** You wouldn't pit your boxer-turned-karate-competitor against the world karate champion in his first match. Likewise, if you can, have the development group start with small projects with low risk and short time frames. After a few of these, the developers will be better prepared to tackle larger, more significant and difficult projects.

This may be a hard sell, but it will pay off in the long run in two ways. First, you will have an outstanding, professional development group skilled in object-oriented development. Second, you will attract and keep the best people, because the best people thrive in an environment such as this one.

Pitfall 1.3: Thinking objects will solve all problems.

The software development process—creating software to solve a particular problem—is long and complex and has many activities and stages. The exact list will vary depending on what book or article you read but can generally be said to include the following:

- becoming aware of and identifying the problem
- deciding to solve the problem
- deciding what resources (time, money, people, mind share, opportunity, authority) to expend solving the problem
- defining the scope of the resulting project and getting it started
- analyzing the problem
- defining the solution
- designing the solution
- implementing the solution
- testing the solution
- verifying that the solution solves the problem in an acceptable manner
- delivering the solution
- modifying and refining the solution to solve new problems or fix existing ones

Far more detail is possible here, including issues of communications, skill level, politics, and user feedback, but you get the idea. And each item has its own set of problems, challenges, and, yes, pitfalls that are quite independent of the development methodology used.

So, here's the problem: How many of these activities will object-oriented development actually affect favorably, especially if you haven't done OOD before? By contrast, how much training and experience will be required to effectively apply appropriate OOD skills in each of these areas?

Symptoms   People who say, in effect, when problems are raised, "Don't worry, we're using object-oriented development; that'll solve this problem." I'm not sure which is more frightening: when nontechnical people say this or when technical people do. As Fred Brooks seems destined to have to prove continually, there is no "silver bullet" to slay the software development monster.

Consequences The project slips or even fails when you discover not only that many problems are not solved by using objects but also that they're made worse by doing so.

Detection Go through the list above and test your own understanding of each of these areas and the challenges they present. Then do the same with all the other key people in the projects at all levels.

Extraction Education of those who misunderstand. This can be difficult if they are upper-management people who have approved projects based on what turn out to be false reassurances. It can be even more difficult if these people have passed on those reassurances to others.

Prevention Establish a process or methodology that takes you through the list above (though not necessarily in a linear fashion; see Pitfall 3.6). List the tasks, resources, and challenges associated with each step. Judge the impact—or lack thereof—that OOD will have in each area. Be especially aware of the investment in training and skill development that will be required at each level as a result of adopting object technology. And, most of all, identify all the problems that OOD will do nothing to solve and may actually make worse.

Pitfall 1.4: Thinking that object technology is mature.

Hey, object-oriented languages have been around for 25 years. All the major compiler vendors offer C++, all the operating systems and environments claim object orientation, computer-aided software engineering (CASE) tools for object methodologies abound, and there are dozens of titles out on object-oriented development, including this one. Everyone, but everyone, is going object-oriented, so it must be proven technology, right?

Wrong. Object technology, as applied to production-grade projects, is still largely a young and somewhat narrow field, especially compared with the well-hammered and heavily used structured development methodologies of the past 25 years—and there are still controversies and arguments over those.

David Howitz, addressing this issue in *Object Magazine*, notes factors that complicate the effort to apply the various proposed object analysis methods to many real-world problems:

- Application boundaries are undefined
- There's often a lack of subject-matter (domain) experts
- The problems to be solved are not deterministic
- Manual (human, extrasystem) activities are important

Howitz notes that this relative lack of breadth and success can lead to serious resistance from experienced MIS managers, who rightly question whether existing object technology can handle all they need to accomplish.

Symptoms Lack of concern over tools to be used; persistent problems integrating tools and methodologies; heavy dependence on tools from a single vendor; having to work around tool and methodology deficiencies.

Consequences Discovery, often late in the schedule, of design and implementation gaps; major schedule slips.

Detection Make a list of all forms of object technology being used in your development effort: methodologies, architectural concepts, CASE tools, languages, diagrams and notations, class libraries, patterns, design and implementation strategies, and so on. Analyze how well they fit together. Get evaluations from all those who use (or should be using) these technologies.

Extraction

After doing the evaluation listed in **Detection**, reset expectations appropriately. Then look for ways to fill the gaps and strengthen the weak spots.

Prevention

For starters, assume that object technology isn't mature and factor that into your project plans. Make a preemptive list of technologies to be used and evaluate ahead of time how stable and comprehensive they are and how well they'll fit together. Fill the gaps ahead of time, either through proper selection or through home-grown solutions.

Pitfall 1.5: Confusing buzzwords with concepts.

It's easy to talk about a project being object-oriented; after all, something called an "object" is involved, so it must be object-oriented, right? Well, no. Just because someone talks about object-oriented technology or even starts using words such as *software components, reuse, polymorphism* and *dynamic binding*, it doesn't mean they know what they're talking about. They may not even *know* that they don't know what they're talking about, because they may not fully understand all the implications and requirements of that concept. It's like the old joke: What's the difference between a computer salesman and a used car salesman? The used car salesman knows how to drive and knows when he's lying.

Symptoms

Constant and unthinking repetition of key words, which are used almost as a mantra to chant problems and difficulties away or to ensure good fortune and product success. Repeated assurances that there will be no extra costs, that you'll get OOD benefits "for free."

Consequences

The most benign consequence—if "benign" is the correct term—is that you don't get the promised benefits but the project gets done anyway. The worst consequence is that the project itself turns out to be infeasible—or, at least, very late and over budget—because those concepts turned out to be critical to project completion or success, even if they weren't understood.

Detection

This pitfall can be difficult to detect for two reasons. First, it requires probing questions and review by someone who really does understand the concepts and who has experience implementing them. The issue then becomes, whom do you trust? If you're technical, you may think that your fellow engineer actually knows what she is talking about; furthermore, in the interests of team unity, you may be unwilling to question or challenge her. If you're not technical, then you're at an even greater disadvantage.

The second problem with detection is that, based on your own experience and technical level, it can be hard to distinguish this situation from the situation in which the person actually does know what she's talking about.

Extraction

At the risk of sounding like a 12-step program, the first thing you must do is to be honest and admit that there may be a problem.

Then get someone from outside the group—preferably someone from outside the company, but at least someone with no ties to group members—to come in and do a project review with the intention of examining the quality of OOD concepts applied to the project. This person must have a sound understanding of object-oriented development principles, must know all the tough questions to ask, and must be willing and able to ask them. If you can't get this done officially (for example, you're an engineer, and your manager doesn't want to face these questions), then see whether you can do the check unofficially.

If the problem turns out to be real, then you get to make a career decision: Raise the red flag, call things to a halt, or push ahead anyway.

Prevention   First, educate yourself and other team members. Read lots of books on object-oriented development (See the reference sections at the end of each chapter of this book, along with the Bibliography.) Read lots of articles in magazines and journals. Attend seminars, if possible. Pass around books, articles, and seminar materials. Ask lots of questions, but be prepared to get pushback from individuals who are insecure in their own understanding.

Second, get or hire experience. Try one or two or three small-scale OOD projects before tackling the large one. Make at least one of those small-scale projects a prototype for your larger, more important project. Hire developers and managers with a proven track record in OOD.

Pitfall 1.6: Confusing tools with principles.

Using object-oriented tools to create an application does not mean that the project will follow solid principles of object-oriented design any more than sitting in (or driving) an Indy class race car qualifies you for the NASCAR circuit.

Many projects written in C++, Object Pascal, and Objective-C reflect no real concept of the principles underlying good design of objects, classes, and domains. In many cases, they reflect no real understanding of professional software engineering in general. Yet using these tools can lead all involved to believe sincerely that they are doing object-oriented development.

Many paths can lead to this situation—upper-level mandates, enthusiastic tool adoption, project rescue attempts—but the root cause is insufficient information and experience.

Symptoms
Engineers, architects, and managers saying, "Of course it's object-oriented: We wrote it using C++!" Beyond that, many of the pitfalls described in this book are indicative, especially those in Chapter 7.

Consequences
For starters, you tend to lose the benefits of object-oriented development: object reuse, reduction in complexity, ease of maintenance, and so on.

Beyond that, the project may actually take longer than it would have if approached as a non-OO project using classic techniques of structured design and information engineering.

Detection
Conduct reviews that ignore the language and focus on the architecture and design aspects of the project. These reviews should focus on class inheritance hierarchy diagrams, class collaboration diagrams, and class interface specifications. See whether anyone actually has these available or can create them on short notice. See whether the diagrams and specifications make sense.

Extraction
If your review turns up serious problems, then halt current development and take the time to evaluate your choices: Either push ahead to completion or rethink, redesign, and reimplement. All the political and financial pressures will point toward the first solution, but it may end up leading to project failure. The second solution is not only more likely to result in a better application it also may get you to completion more quickly.

Prevention   Education and experience are the keys. First, the key designers and architects should have a solid grounding in principles of object-oriented analysis and design. Ideally, they should have actual experience, but if your group is just converting to OO approaches, you may end up in a "learning by doing" situation. Second, the implementers (who may be the same people) should likewise have training or experience (or both) in object-oriented design and programming.

Pitfall 1.7: Confusing presentation with methodology.

The previous pitfall (1.6) talked about development efforts being labeled "object-oriented" because they happened to be written in an object-oriented programming language. It can get worse than that.

Products, projects, and applications are sometimes considered object-oriented because they have one or more of the following attributes:

- They use a graphical user interface with windows and menus.
- They have icons on the screen that the user can drag around.
- They use an event-driven approach.
- They are broken up into modules.
- They create libraries which can be reused.
- They are part of a client/server or distributed application.
- They pass messages to other tasks or applications.
- They allow data from one application to be embedded within a document created by another.

None of these attributes inherently has anything to do with object-oriented design and implementation; all of them can be implemented using procedural engineering. (Heck, we implemented the first five back in 1984 in the SunDog game mentioned in the Introduction.)

Symptoms   Use of the term "object-oriented" in a way that doesn't seem to make sense. Undue focus (positive or negative) on how the application looks.

Consequences   Mild to severe miscommunication, with all its attendant ills, including misdirected efforts. The worst consequence is wrong expectations for the results of your efforts, with the resulting impact on planning and delivery.

Detection   If you suspect that someone has fallen into this pit, ask her or him to define what exactly they think "object-oriented" means. Probe until you are convinced that the person understands the concepts of objects, classes, inheritance, instantiation, abstraction, encapsulation, and so on. If you keep getting talk about the items above, you may have trouble.

Extraction

Prepare a presentation on what "object-oriented development" does and does not mean. Without stepping on too many toes, illustrate which misconceptions may be floating around. Explain whether the project actually is object-oriented and what (if anything) can be done to make it so.

Prevention

Carry out the **Detection** and **Extraction** phases before the project gets off the ground. Explain just what it will mean if this project is to be truly "object oriented." Point out the costs, the risks, the requirements, and the benefits. If expectations are centered on the attributes listed above, treat them as requirements or requests that are separate from the project's object orientation.

Pitfall 1.8: Confusing training with skill.

Training is the acquisition of information and practices geared toward a certain end. For example, send a group of engineers to a conference with seminars on object technology, hold a class on C++ programming, or give them a set of books and other materials on object-oriented development. If they're bright and experienced, they'll grasp the concepts readily and start applying them, and you're ready to push ahead. Right?

Well, maybe not. You see, knowledge and even understanding are not the same as skill. Skill comes from experience; it is the ability to use knowledge wisely and effectively. A programmer who has Smalltalk or C++ or Eiffel or CLOS syntax down cold still may not know how best to program in that language, the standard idioms, and common errors or pitfalls to avoid.

Going up one level from the language, knowing how to program effectively in a given object-oriented programming language doesn't guarantee skill in the implementation of object classes or in class hierarchies. And skill in those areas doesn't automatically translate into skill in object analysis and design.

Symptoms   Managers who say, "Of course we can do object-oriented development; we've sent all our engineers to seminars!" Engineers who say, "Yeah, I'm sure I can pick up C++ quickly."

Consequences   The best consequence is that the developers will realize that they need to develop—or are developing—skills and will adjust their efforts and estimates appropriately. The worst consequence is that no one will recognize or admit the lack of skill, and the project will limp along, slip constantly, or crash spectacularly.

Detection   Ask your engineers and architects to rate and briefly document their skills, talents, and experience—not just their knowledge—in the following areas:

- object analysis methodologies
- object design methodologies
- class hierarchy design
- object class design

- object class implementation
- language skills, particularly features and pitfalls

Then have them rate one another. Then rate them yourself.

Extraction

If the project is small in scale, is not critical, or is close to completion, push ahead and finish it. Use it as an opportunity to develop the skills of all the people involved. If, however, the project appears to be at risk and is too important, you may need to do a schedule reset and bring in people (consultants or contractors) who have the required skills.

Prevention

Skills come only with time and effort. There's an old aphorism that says: Good judgment comes from experience; experience comes from poor judgment. Substitute "skill" for "judgment," and you get the idea of the process. Stephen Covey (in *The Seven Habits of Highly Effective People*) talks about the Law of the Harvest, referring to our inability to force a crop of wheat to grow overnight or even in a few days.

However, this doesn't mean that you have to start from the ground floor and build your way slowly. First, find (in-house) or hire (from outside) talent and skill so that you start with people who have a better idea of what to do and how to do it. Next, have them act as mentors, with the other developers as apprentices. The apprentice-journeyman-master system evolved over centuries and has much to recommend it in a profession as craft- and skill-intensive as software engineering. Unfortunately, the short-term focus of most firms doing software development precludes or, at least, hinders that kind of long-term investment.

What if you can't find or hire skill? Then you'll have to pay for it in time. Invest in training and use a series of projects, starting small and growing larger, to develop and hone the skills.

Pitfall 1.9: Confusing prototypes with finished products.

Make no mistake: Object-oriented development combined with powerful user-interface classes and tools can greatly speed application development. However, they also allow application prototypes to be put together and demonstrated very quickly. This is great for examining and testing various user interfaces, or for conveying the essential nature of the application being developed.

But there is a drawback to this speed of prototyping. People not involved in development—notably, upper management, investors, and customers—consciously or unconsciously see the application as being closer to completion than it is. They find it hard to understand why the rest of development should take so long, not realizing that what they're seeing may not have any code that is actually used in the final product.

Symptoms   A good clue for starters is someone not involved in development saying, "I don't see why it's taking so long; after all, you demonstrated the product [or a particular feature] to me several months ago." Less-direct indications include issues of effort or competence or both being raised about the development team. For a more subtle, management-oriented variation on this, see Pitfall 3.9.

Consequences   Suspicion from nondevelopers that the development team isn't working as hard as it could or is somehow incompetent. Loss of trust and credibility.

Detection   If you have reason to suspect that this is happening (due to symptoms or gut feelings), start asking for explicit feedback from the nondevelopers you're concerned about. Here's a good question: "Based on what you've seen so far, when do you think we'll be ready to ship?"

Extraction   You absolutely must reset expectations and get the nondevelopers in sync with reality. The question mentioned above in **Detection** is a good place to start. Follow up by asking questions about how long the person thinks each of the yet-incomplete features or aspects should take to finish. Be sure to raise every single feature or aspect you can think of as well as noting completion dependencies. And don't forget to point out the time it will take to debug, test, and verify all these features.

You need to ask them how long they think it will take because non-developers often have unconscious assumptions and expectations, which when dragged out into sunlight and examined, quickly shrivel and fade away. Left unexamined, however, they become a constant and unstoppable source of frustration, causing those people to be dissatisfied with whatever progress you're making.

Prevention The best solution: Don't show prototypes to those not involved in development except possibly to potential customers doing testing and evaluation. Politically and financially, that restriction is not always feasible. If you must show prototypes, go to great lengths to set proper expectations ahead of time.

Be sure to indicate all the work that remains to be done. Show every area that is incomplete or nonfunctional. Be conservative (that is, pessimistic) about the amount of time required to fully implement and test each feature. In short, make the prototype sound even more worthless than it is; you are always better off underpromising and overdelivering than the other way around.

Conclusions

In some respects, these pitfalls are the most serious in object-oriented development. First, they can be among the hardest to detect. Second, they can be among the hardest to extract yourself from or to avoid. Third, they can cost you your job, whether you're in them or fighting to get out of them.

Three core problems may occur:

- Upper management and customers have unrealistic expectations and demands, and they do not trust technical management and developers to be honest when they say how long something should take to complete.

- Technical management, already struggling to get realistic timetables accepted and sufficient resources to meet them, feels overwhelmed by having to deal with OOD-specific issues as well, much less asking for additional time and resources to resolve them properly.

- Developers become enthusiastic about OOD, see quick results, and never complete their OOD education. Indeed, they may resist it, feeling they already understand "all that." In the process, they may feel that they don't have time or need for meticulous design and implementation.

Note that these three problems all have roots independent of object-oriented development, but the introduction of OOD exacerbates the existing tendencies. A company in which upper management, technical management, and developers are all working together—using realistic schedules, on-going education, and solid engineering techniques—will likely have the fewest problems and gain the most benefits from adopting OOD.

References

Brooks, Frederick P., Jr. "No silver bullet: essence and accidents of software engineering." *Computer,* Vol. 20, No. 4, April 1987.

Covey, Stephen. *The Seven Habits of Highly Effective People.* New York: Simon & Schuster Inc., 1990.

Howitz, David. "Bringing objects to mainstream MIS." *Object Magazine,* Vol. 2, No. 4; Nov/Dec 1992.

Page-Jones, Meiler. "Object orientation: the importance of being earnest." *Object Magazine*, Vol. 2, No. 2; Jul/Aug 1992.

CHAPTER 2:

POLITICAL PITFALLS

...there is nothing more difficult to carry out, nor more doubtful of success, nor more danger-ous to handle, than to initiate a new order of things. For the reformer has enemies in all those who profit by the old order, and only lukewarm defenders in all those who would profit by the new order, this lukewarmness arising partly from fear of their adversaries...and partly from the incredulity of mankind, who do not truly believe in anything new until they have had actual experience of it.

—Niccolo Machiavelli, *The Prince*

Political pitfalls are perhaps the most treacherous, because they have little to do with skill, technology, or the worthwhile nature of a given project. Instead, they have to do with credit, blame, power, control, promotion, personalities, gossip, image, past slights, called favors, sabotage, championing, and tradition. Developers and other technical types are prone to blunder into political pitfalls because developers like to think of themselves as rational technocrats and assume that others will think as they do and be motivated as they are.

At the same time, it is a common error on the part of upper management to think that developers and other technical types are naive or ignorant about organizational politics. Developers are often very astute and aware of politics, but they find it disgusting and destructive (rightfully so) and tend to dismiss it as not worth considering (wrongly so). This tends to play into the hands of upper management, who feel that they have every-thing well in hand. They don't realize the real danger they face from a group of ticked-off developers who decide to "hack" politics: that is, to use (and abuse) organizational politics to achieve an end. Many mid-level managers (and some high-level ones) have found their power base eroded and have even found themselves out of a job because of developer sabotage or rebellion, whether overt or covert.

The point is that organizational politics does exist, it is significant, and it can be ignored only at the peril of your project and possibly your job. The pitfalls listed here are those you are most likely to fall into when attempting to initiate or promote the use of object-oriented development within your organization.

Pitfall 2.1: Not educating and enlisting management before the fact.

There is an oft-cited dictum in technology development groups: "It is easier to beg forgiveness than ask permission." In fact, it was a motto of pioneer programmer Admiral Grace Hopper. It is often true and sometimes crucial to circumvent bureaucratic foot-dragging and politics. But it is not always the best course, and the danger of following it is commensurate with the technical, financial, and political risks involved. And all three risks abound when an organization is moving to object-oriented development for the first time.

Nevertheless, it is not uncommon for a development group to make the switch to OOD with only minimal involvement and education of upper management. Indeed, management may not care very much or may even be supportive—having read an article about the wonders of object technology in a weekly business magazine.

And that is where the pitfall lies. For unless the project comes in within acceptable time and budget limits, upper management will suddenly be asking hard questions reflecting reasonable or unreasonable expectations, given what they know or were told.

Symptoms   Apparent lack of knowledge or overly positive expectations or both on the part of management about OOD and its role in the relevant projects. Sudden distancing or self-protecting activities if problems crop up.

Consequences   Lack of support and possibly active hostility from upper management if problems arise or if their expectations aren't met. Finding yourself twisting in the wind. Career damage, lack of promotion, demotion, loss of job.

Detection   Sit down with upper management and find out how much they understand about object technology and how it's being applied in the relevant project(s). Have them detail their expectations. Find out their level of enthusiasm or concern for the use of OOD.

Extraction   There's little to do except start the education and enrollment process much later than it should have been. It may be really tough, depending on how current expectations compare to reality, and the truth is, there's no good reason for not having done this before things got started.

Prevention   From the pitfall itself, it's obvious that there are two separate (if related) tasks: educating and enlisting. The first comprises letting management know exactly what OOD entails, which means that you had better know yourself, and you'd better know it well enough to explain it to nontechnical people. Work to contain your own enthusiasm for OOD; remember that it is safer to underpromise and overdeliver.

Second, and this is probably tougher, you need to enlist key people: those who can affect your budget and resources, and those who can affect the scope and direction of your project. If you can, prove yourself with small projects to establish credibility and to give your sponsors a track record to point to (and take credit for).

Pitfall 2.2: Underestimating the resistance.

Objects are wonderful. At least, *you* think they are, based on anything from a breathless magazine article to years of experience with solid, successful object-oriented development. Or you may not think they're wonderful, but you do think they may offer advantages and benefits to your development efforts. And, of course, what's obvious to you should be obvious—or, at least, understandable—to everyone else.

So you blithely push ahead...until people start pushing back. And before you know it, you're engaged in a political battle, fighting resistance to object technology that may range from guerrilla sniping to a full frontal assault.

Why might people resist accepting object technology? The reasons are varied and may range from the well-founded to the completely irrational to the deliberately obstructionist. Here are examples:

- They don't understand object technology.
- They don't want to understand object technology.
- They're afraid they won't be able to understand object technology (and thus will have less value to the company).
- They know they won't be able to understand object technology, because they've been sloughing for the last ten years and know that this will expose them for what they are.
- They have very strong feelings about the language and/or programming methodology, or tools or all three that they currently use.
- They really detest the language, methodology, or tools or all three that you're proposing they use.
- They're worried that the reasons for adopting object technology aren't well thought through.
- They're worried that the plan for adopting object technology has significant problems or flaws.
- They want to adopt object technology, but they want to do it their way.
- They want you to fail so that they (or someone they like better) can get your job.
- They read this book.

Compounding the situation is the fact that you may face several of the reasons simultaneously, possibly from different sources.

Symptoms   Delays in getting approval or support. Rumors circulating behind your back. Objections constantly brought up in meetings. Former supporters distancing themselves from you. Reduction in project priority and resources.

Consequences   Significant project delays or project failure. Loss of influence. Loss of job.

Detection   If you suspect that resistance is deeper or more entrenched than you thought, you need to find out the sources of resistance and the reasons behind it. This can be hard, because the people resisting you may not be honest about what they're doing, or why they're doing it.

Furthermore, if the resistance is coming from above, your boss(es) may feel no obligation to explain their reasons.

Extraction   You have four choices, not necessarily mutually exclusive, based on the nature, depth, and source of the resistance:

- Push ahead in spite of it.
- Mollify or enlist those who resist.
- Redirect the project to quell the objections.
- Abandon the project gracefully and (maybe) try again later.

Prevention   Make a list of everyone who might have any input or influence and judge where they stand. If possible, meet with each one privately to sound out her or him—but recognize that you may not get an honest answer. Offer each person a chance to make criticisms and recommendations; let everyone feel a part of the project and the process. Build enthusiasm, pointing out specific benefits, particularly those of interest to each individual. Use each source to cross-check others. This process is known as "getting your ducks in a row," and you'd better do that before you start. This process may be more critical for those below you than those above you; don't underestimate the power of developers to make your life wonderful or miserable (see this chapter's introduction as well as Pitfall 3.2).

Having done that, assess the costs and risks in pushing this project forward compared to the possible benefits and rewards. Factor that with the probability of success and make your call. If it looks too dangerous, scale back or redirect. If it looks impossible, find somewhere else to work.

Pitfall 2.3: Overselling the technology.

It's easy to get excited about object-oriented development. It works very well for small-scale projects. It has real benefits for managing complexity. It builds very well on what we've learned about software engineering over the past 25 years. It is an important—and perhaps an essential—part of solving the growing software development crisis.

Enthusiasm for object technology, particularly for individuals relatively new at it or with a vested interest in its adoption, may lead them to give glowing descriptions of its wonders and benefits to you and others.

Object proponents may make these comments in all sincerity and innocence. Or they may make them with the knowledge that they are stretching the truth a bit or perhaps rupturing it altogether. But whether they know that what they're saying is accurate is, to a point, immaterial: When reality intrudes, the results will be the same, and their lack of knowledge or their lack of accuracy will convict them equally.

Symptoms   There are two phases. First, those who have been oversold express expectations of the object technology that make you increasingly uncomfortable; you may find yourself starting to downplay things a bit. Second, as problems start to pile up, there are growing questions, doubts, and expressions of mistrust and cynicism.

Consequences   Those who trusted what they were told will feel betrayed; those who did not will feel justified. In either case, both the reputation and the influence of those doing the overselling will shrink, and it will be a long, hard road to recovery.

Detection   Sit down with a sheet of paper and write every promise, hope, and expectation that you or others have made in the name of object-oriented development. Ask yourself how supportable or valid each is. If you have questions about your ability to judge this, find someone who knows more about OOD than you do and ask them for help evaluating how supportable or valid each point is. Ask yourself whether you've succumbed to wishful thinking.

Extraction   If you or others have oversold the technology, you need to start readjusting expectations immediately. It is probably best to do it in one massive reset than to do it piecemeal—a single sword thrust is, in the end, less painful than a thousand paper cuts. But it's going to take a long time to reestablish your credibility.

Prevention   Several times in this book you will find the recommendation to underpromise and overdeliver. Believe it and make sure that others believe it. If you have questions about your ability to judge, then bring in two or three experts to consult and weigh their opinions.

On the other hand, if you knowingly oversell, telling yourself that you can manage things down the road, you will almost certainly be wrong. Resist that temptation. It will always get you into trouble, and your own integrity will be diminished. It's just not worth it.

Pitfall 2.4: Getting religious about object-oriented development.

Let's try to keep our perspective while standing knee-deep in the hoopla. As anyone experienced in this area will tell you, object-oriented development is not going to end world hunger or bring about peace in our time. It won't transform the country of your choice into the new economic superpower of the 21st century. It won't end cancer, reduce the number of handgun deaths, or curb the rate of out-of-wedlock births. It won't even affect dandruff.

Closer to home, OOD doesn't invalidate existing programming languages, methodologies, and tools. It won't make good engineers or architects out of bad ones. It also won't make good products out of bad ones; although it may allow you to write a better program than you might have otherwise, you can write awful programs just as well using object technology as you can using, say, BASIC or Cobol or your favorite scapegoat.

Switching to object technology probably won't make a late project ship on time, though it may allow you to complete a project that never would have shipped otherwise. On the other hand, it may make the project even later. OOD won't have a major impact on the time and effort required for analysis, design, and testing—except, possibly, to increase it. You won't be able to reuse 90 percent (or 60 percent or probably even 30 percent or maybe even 10 percent) of the code from your first project. OOD may not even be the best solution to a given problem. It might, in fact, make things worse, not better.

Symptoms   An almost blind faith in the virtues of OOD and an equal blindness to its pitfalls and failings.

Consequences   Arguments with others; a lack of flexibility; blindness to weak spots.

Detection   Analyze reactions to each of the statements above. When people disagree, note any strong negative emotional response. Have those who disagree with a given statement explain it to a disinterested, yet knowledgeable third party and see whether they think the logic holds water.

Extraction   As with many pitfalls, study and experience will do much to cure this one. Beyond that, the **Detection** method above will help you to identify specific areas of excess enthusiasm and credulity.

Prevention   Read the books in the Bibliography. Find people who have completed meaningful projects using OOD and ask them for their lessons learned. Have them read the opening paragraphs of this pitfall and respond to any items they disagree with.

Pitfall 2.5: Not recognizing the politics of architecture.

Once, while discussing the challenges of object-oriented development with Taligent trainer Tom Affinito, I mentioned—citing Fred Brooks—the need for a chief architect (see Pitfalls 4.13 and 4.14). Tom immediately responded, "Yes, and ultimately architecture is a political act."

Unless you are both sole architect and sole implementor—and maybe even then—architecture is a political act, and it is especially true in development groups of any size. Developers like to think themselves above politics. Not so; they are as human as anyone else. Developers can be quite political and will use a variety of techniques, good and bad, to achieve their ends: persuasion, hyperbole, fear-mongering, caucusing, lobbying, consensus building, rumors, backbiting, leadership, intimidation, sacrifice, tantrums, threats, and subversion, to name a few. The fact that developers are generally very bright just increases the effectiveness of whatever techniques they use.

Architecture is the lodestar of developer politics because it is ultimately the most prestigious role in software development. Brooks goes to great lengths (and rightfully so) to assert the intellectual and creative challenges of implementation, but it is Frank Lloyd Wright's name that remains attached to the structures he designed, not the name of the contractors who built them. Or, to update an old programming joke, the verb "to develop" is conjugated this way: "I architect, you implement, he tests."

Yet we may fail to recognize or acknowledge this situation and its implications. Why? First, we want to believe that all developers have (with regard to the project) the same intentions and goals. Second, we want to believe that the best course is the one that is obvious to us and that everyone else will agree with that. Third, we don't want to have to deal with politics ourselves, particularly politics that can lead to confrontations.

Symptoms Assuming that all other developers have the same goals, ideas, and talents. Not wanting to assert architectural issues. Finger-pointing as design problems arise.

Consequences Hidden or overt team dissension, leading to poor morale and lack of cooperation as well as a weakened architecture.

Detection   Ask yourself these questions:

- Who is the chief architect of this project?
- How well do the other developers support the chief architect?
- How effective is the chief architect in her role?
- What are the obstacles she faces?
- What are all the political issues involved?

Answering these questions should go a long way toward determining whether you have underestimated the politics of architecture.

Extraction   The first issue to address is that of authority commensurate with responsibility: If there is a chief architect on the team, does she really have the authority to compel adherence to the architecture? This kind of authority is different than being able to say, "Do this or you're off the project," which often leads to subtle or overt rebellion by team members. This kind of authority accrues from several factors:

- a proven track record
- respect from teammates
- upport from technical and upper management
- a mutual pact with the developers that the chief architect will give serious consideration to all their ideas and suggestions but that they will abide by her decisions
- a willingness to give in on the small things so that she can hold her ground on the big things

Beyond that, healing a team that is experiencing jealousy and dissension is no easy feat, especially when you're in the middle of a project. Books and seminars on team-building abound; study, learn, and apply.

Prevention   Go through the questions in **Detection** but cast them in the future tense. Then, as with **Extraction**, proactively work to build the team and establish the authority of the chief architect.

Pitfall 2.6: Getting on the feature-release treadmill.

You know the drill. By hook or crook, through long weeks and late hours and ruthless compromising, you finally deliver the project. It's finished, it's out the door, and you have taken a few weeks to remind yourself what real life is like. Now you have the opportunity to go back and make right all the hacks and shortcuts and ugly patches you used to get version 1.0 of the project to the customers. Besides, having done the project once, you now have a far better idea of how it should have been done in the first place. You rub your hands together and...

...you are handed a list of new features required by customers or potential customers for version 2.0 of the project, which has to ship far sooner than you would have thought. After some study, you realize that you're not going to be able to deliver all those features within the required time frame—and even as you realize that, more features get handed down.

Your plans for cleaning up the code and the architecture are rapidly getting pushed off to version 3.0, and you really wonder whether things will be any different then.

Chances are, they won't.

Why does this happen so often? There are several reasons, really. One may be economic necessity. Your company (division, group) may have to fund itself, which means that sales have to be sufficient to meet all expenses, including your salary and benefits. This is especially true in the lean and mean decade of the 1990s, when, as one wag has put it, the new status symbol is a job. If that's your situation, then don't worry as much about this pitfall; architectural purity is nice, but a paycheck is better.

Another, less acceptable reason may be a short-term focus on the part of upper management. Determined to milk a current market opportunity and concerned primarily about next quarter's results, they may not be receptive to an engineering investment that would yield more in the long run at the expense of smaller profits right now.

A third reason—not necessarily exclusive of the other two, and sometimes justified—is a suspicion on the part of upper management that engineers are more interested in doing something "cool" or "elegant" than in doing something profitable. What upper management may not understand is that elegance—architecture and code that are concise, yet clear and comprehensive, tending toward orthogonality—always pays off. Always. The only question is how soon and how much, and that is the fulcrum for the balancing act of the technical manager. Ironically, when the engineering staff is able to rapidly deliver the features requested by upper management, it is often because of a previous investment in elegance; likewise, when features take a long time to implement or bugs take a long time to fix, it's often because of architectural gaps and past short-cuts.

Symptoms   Constantly having to push engineering work into the next planned release and not the current one.

Consequences   The cost of adding new features or extending current ones goes up, not down, over time. The program gets larger, less stable, and less cohesive. Bugs multiply, possibly causing a customer backlash.

Detection   Sit down with upper management and detail the engineering work that needs to be done. Indicate what impact this will have on the current list of desired features. See what kind of reaction you get.

Extraction   It ain't easy. The reaction you get under **Detection** should give you a pretty good idea of what things will be like. There are two approaches, which should probably be used together. First, actively work with upper management and customers to determine which features are absolutely necessary and which are merely desirable —ones they could live without until the next feature release. It's critical to talk directly with the customers, because they may not have done their own prioritizing; the list you get from management may reflect everything from essential requirements to blue-sky wishes.

Second, build engineering cleanup time into each feature so that an engineer allocated four weeks for a given feature spends, say, three weeks on the feature and one week on architecture.

Prevention   Besides using the steps described above in **Extraction,** you need to sell the legitimate, long-term benefits of object-oriented development and emphasize the need to make the proper ongoing engineering investment in order to get those benefits. This means investing the time to educate management and customers, to set proper expectations, and (if possible) to run a trial project to demonstrate the process.

Pitfall 2.7: Betting the company on objects.

Imagine the following scene. Your company's executive staff gathers for a presentation on a new technology that will revolutionize information productivity. After a presentation citing the ongoing problems of information management, enterprise computing, and competitive response, you are presented with the solution that will boost the company's bottom line and guarantee its future: structured development!

But wait! you say. Structured development has been around for a long time. Lots of folks use structured development and have mixed results; indeed, most don't use it well. Lots of companies have gone out of business while relying upon structured development. How is structured development going to guarantee our future?

Good question. And yet, structured development and its associated methodologies are more mature, established, and well understood in real-world applications than are object-oriented development and its methodologies. For that matter, the number of competent, practicing engineers who are expert at structured development is vastly greater than the number of competent, practicing engineers who are expert at object-oriented development. If a company can't succeed using structured development, why does it think it can succeed using OOD?

You may think that I'm being reactionary or that I don't understand all the benefits OOD has over structured development. If so, you miss the point: It is not *technique* (using Jacques Ellul's term) in and of itself that will benefit the company, but rather its intelligent and purposeful application by people who know what they're doing and why. To think that adoption of object technology will suddenly make everything better is irrational to the point of superstition.

Symptoms

Unrealistic expectations on the part of upper management. Marketers overpromising delivery times and feature lists. Technical managers who see object technology as a silver bullet. Developers neglecting solid software engineering practices, because "objects don't require them."

Consequences

At best, you go through a wrenching reeducation and attitude adjustment. At worst, you lose the bet.

Detection   Take the company's current business plan, mission statement, and product plans, and eliminate all references to and consideration of object technology. Do all of these documents still all make sense?

Extraction   Point out, repeatedly, that it doesn't matter what technology you use if the products aren't worthwhile and if the company can't get a return on investment. Enumerate the factors required for success independent of object technology. Look at all that you can do to maximize those factors. Then—and only then—look at how object-oriented development can aid and support those efforts.

Prevention   Bet the company on people, not on objects. Isn't that what politics is all about?

Conclusion

The term *politics*, like *politician*, has gained a patina—maybe a crust—of oil and mud. The very term carries a reek of manipulation, dissembling, power seeking, battle lines, patronage, and self-aggrandizement at the expense of others. I suspect that more companies falter and fail due to the consequences of internal politics than for any other reason.

But the obverse of that coin has writ on it leadership, consensus building, mutual loyalty, team spirit, and self-sacrifice for the common good. Cynics smirk at such concepts in a business setting, deriding them as naive at best and deceptive manipulation at worst. Yet these impulses are as valid as those above and are more likely to lead to success.

It is a sad commentary on human nature that office politics partake too much of the former and not enough of the latter. But it is a true observation, and so be aware of and beware of the political pitfalls that abound.

References

Ellul, Jacques. *The Technological Society*. New York: Vintage Books, 1964.

Machiavelli, Niccolo. *The Prince* and *The Discourses*. New York: Random House, 1950. (Translated by John Wilkinson).

CHAPTER 3:

MANAGEMENT PITFALLS

I will govern according to the common weal, but not according to the common will.
— King James I of England (1621)

Technical managers are the women and men in the middle. They serve as a buffer between the requirements of upper management and the efforts of developers. When things work out well, it's a wonderful job; but when problems arise, it can seem pretty thankless. Technical management is a job that offers strong temptations to err in different directions.

The pitfalls in this chapter deal specifically with technical management of object-oriented development projects. They tend to be rooted in three general temptations:

- wanting to look good to and get along with upper management
- wanting to trust that your developers are doing as well as they tell you they are
- wanting to believe that things are progressing as fast as they appear to be

Managers and developers often assume that using OOD will eliminate, or at least ease, various development bottlenecks. That may very well happen but only with sufficient education in OOD techniques and issues as well as *increased* discipline in software engineering practices.

In short, object-oriented development requires more discipline, more management, and more training than classic software engineering does. But if you see to these needs and avoid the pitfalls in this chapter, the payoff will be much greater.

Pitfall 3.1: Adopting objects without well-defined objectives.

One of the defining moments in American politics during the past 25 years occurred early in the 1980 presidential campaign. Senator Ted Kennedy, heir apparent to Camelot, was challenging his party's incumbent, Jimmy Carter, for the nomination. Carter was seen as vulnerable to a Republican challenger, so Kennedy was ready to step up to the legacy of his two martyred brothers. Whatever his past troubles, he was still considered a shoo-in for the Democratic nomination and a credible response to the Republicans.

Then, one evening during a live interview on a CBS news program, Roger Mudd asked Kennedy why he wanted to be president. For only a minute or two—but must have seemed like an eternity—Kennedy struggled inarticulately, unable to utter a coherent sentence, much less a compelling, thoughtful response. It seemed that either the question had never occurred to him or he was unwilling to express his true reasons and unable to come up with an acceptable substitute on a moment's notice. Whatever the case, his support peaked at that moment and slid downward from there. He lost the nomination to Carter, who in turn lost the election to Ronald Reagan.

What's the point? Just this: If you're going to adopt object technology, be sure you know exactly why you're doing it and what you hope to get out of it. It is not uncommon for development groups to decide to move into object technology because it is a Good Thing; yet they fail to establish what exactly they expect to get out of it. "Faster development," "greater flexibility," and "code reuse" are nice phrases, but so are "the flag," "motherhood," and "apple pie." Many groups explore object technology because it's interesting and new. A pilot project may be well defined—for example, the creation of a simple custom application—but often no clear follow-up exists.

Symptoms   Lack of measurable progress; lack of defined deliverables; lack of understanding as to what comes next.

Consequences Loss of focus and direction; pilot projects seem to drag on forever; real projects are constantly redefined.

Detection   Describe in writing the ideal state of object-oriented development in your firm in, say, two to five years (depending upon the size of your company and team). If this is hard to do, or if what you write seems vague, then you have a good indication that you've fallen into this pitfall.

Once you are satisfied with this statement, then describe in detail—*working backward from your long-term goal*—each of the steps to get you from where you are now to where you want to be. If you run into gaps or leaps of faith, then you know you're facing this pitfall.

Extraction   Follow the process in **Detection**: work *backward* from your long-term goal in a series of steps, filling in any gaps that you encounter. Be very about identifying and defining the objectives for each step.

Prevention   Follow the process described in **Detection** and **Extraction**. You may end up deciding that your long-term goal is unrealistic; if so, adjust it. Remember that conditions will likely change over three to five years, so make sure that you aren't locked into that single goal. Instead, make sure that at each step or phase, you have a chance to re-evaluate or reset the eventual goal and shift accordingly.

Pitfall 3.2: Cramming objects down the developers' throats.

In a sense, this is the complement of Pitfall 2.1 (not educating and enlisting management before the fact). Someone—a senior executive, a technical manager (perhaps you), a project leader, a senior programmer—becomes convinced that objects are the way to go and so mandates that object technology be adopted.

This can happen for a variety of reasons. The person may be genuinely convinced that objects are the way to go, that they will make the developers' jobs easier. He may be worried about a competitor who is (or isn't) using objects. He may be struggling with missed deadlines and see this as a way to better predict software development costs and risks. Or he may simply want to extract the last erg of productivity out of the developers.

Whatever the intent, the backlash can be disastrous.

Symptoms   Resistance from developers. Grumblings and complaints. Mysterious bugs.

Consequences   Missed deadlines. Project failure. Open revolt.

Detection   Sit down with each developer (or a representative sample) and ask them the following questions. Recognize that—depending on your relationship with them and the political situation at work—it may be hard to get an honest answer:

- What do you see as the benefits of adopting (having adopted) object technology?

- Do you see areas of concern? What are they?

- How do you feel the transition to object-oriented development should be (is being, has been) handled?

- How would you do things differently?

These questions aren't exactly earthshaking, but many managers fail to ask such questions of their developers. By their answers, you should be able to gauge the level of discontent (if any) among the developers. Ask yourself the same questions, and see how your answers correspond to those of your developers.

Extraction

First, go through the **Detection** phase. Asking these questions will not only help you see whether there is a problem, but it will also give you some possible solutions and can help make the developers a part of the solution.

Next, hold team or group meetings on the subject, using the responses to help put together an agenda. Depending on how much emotion is involved, you may need to be very careful to keep the meeting from turning into a finger-pointing or dumping session. Listen carefully and take notes; again, you should get many ideas about possible answers from this meeting.

Finally, reintroduce objects based on developer feedback. Get the developers involved so that they feel that their comments and efforts are useful and that they have an investment in object technology.

Prevention

The **Detection/Extraction** sequence can be used to avoid this pitfall in the first place. Be prepared to face opposition, to listen to it, and to consider it well. After all, the developers may have valid and critical reasons that object technology should be adopted slowly (if at all); look at the pitfalls in this book.

Pitfall 3.3: Abandoning good software engineering practices.

Why would the use of object-oriented development cause managers and developers to neglect or even abandon solid software engineering practices? Those practices are under pressure from the start. Many engineers don't know them and aren't willing to spend (or aren't given) the time to learn them. Those who do know them often aren't willing to spend (or aren't given) the time to practice them. Technical managers, who often do understand such techniques, find themselves caught in a vise, trapped between ever-increasing (and possibly unrealistic) demands of upper management and the productivity level of the engineers they supervise.

The introduction of object-oriented development can cause a new set of problems. Upper management, having read articles about the benefits of OOD, may see it as an opportunity to increase demands. Developers, already under pressure to produce, milk the benefits of OOD for all they're worth and may find even less incentive to focus on solid software engineering. And the technical managers in the middle have to cope with the specifics of OOD while still fighting the software engineering battles.

Symptoms   Upper management unwilling to allocate the necessary time and resources for design up front and for testing following development. Engineers doing class and object design on the fly. Neglect of solid engineering within class methods. Engineers unwilling to adhere to design and coding standards and protocols.

Consequences   Poor design on all levels (domain, class, object); poor fit among objects; lots and lots of bugs, dragging out testing time; late or canceled projects.

Detection   It's usually not hard to detect the pressure from upper management; indeed, the problem is resisting the pressure. As for the engineering-level problems, the best detection comes from regular code reviews in which the engineer discusses and defends the design and implementation decisions for each given object class.

Extraction   This pitfall is a hard one to get out of, because upper management needs to allocate more time and resources, and the engineers need the self-discipline and education to change how they're doing things. The key is to educate everyone about the benefits of good software engineering practices: established practices, predictable schedules, and higher quality.

Prevention

It is sad that there is often so much resistance to doing things right in the first place. The approach is direct: realistic scheduling, definition of engineering standards, and enforcement of engineering practices. For starters, make everyone—especially upper management—read *The Mythical Man-Month* by Frederick P. Brooks. Then refer to it again and again as these problems arise.

Pitfall 3.4: Not defining and using an effective methodology.

What exactly is a methodology? It is the collection of practices, notations, steps, and approaches used to manage and direct the software development life cycle. The phases in that life cycle are themselves warmly debated, and they can vary in definition and relationship in each given methodology. In the simplest of terms, software development consists of:

- **analysis:** deciding what problem(s) need to be solved and gathering data and requirements about them
- **design:** solving the problems based on the data and requirements
- **implementation:** realizing the solution using the systems (hardware, software, physical, human) at hand
- **revision:** improving and refining the analysis, design, or implementation based on new and cumulative experience

Many methodologies exist specifically for object-oriented development. Among them are Booch, Coad and Yourdon, Colbert, Fusion (Coleman *et al.*), MERODE, OMT (Rumbaugh *et al.*), OORASS (Reenskaug), OOSD (Wasserman *et al.*), OOSE (Jacobson *et al.*), OSMOSYS (Winter Partners), RRD/CRC (Beck, Wirfs-Brock, *et al.*), Shlaer/Mellor, SOMA, and Texel, to name some but not all.

Many developers of object-oriented development projects, faced with a bewildering set of options and no clear means of choosing among them, adopt no methodology at all and push ahead by the seat of their pants. Or they pick one but get bogged down in using it, because of a lack of effective tools, inherent limitations in the methodology, or both.

Symptoms   A development process that seems to lurch from crisis to crisis, with milestones and deadlines that slip ever further out of reach.

Consequences   Products that solve the wrong problems. Designs that can't be implemented. Massive schedule slips.

Detection   For starters, ask yourself and others these questions:

- What's our development methodology? How well defined is it? How universally is it understood, used, and followed in the development group?

- What analysis did we do? What written information and diagrams did the analysis produce?

- What designing did we do? What written information and diagrams did the design produce?

- How comprehensive were our analysis and design efforts before we started implementation? Did we have all the required information? How many times did we have to go back to repeat our analysis and design?

- Do we expect to do analysis, design, and implementation only once before shipping?

The answers to these questions should give you a good idea as to whether you methodology is effective, if you have one at all.

Extraction   Put things on hold for a few days to focus everyone on the need for a methodology. Use the results of the **Detection** exercise to define gaps and flaws in your current approach. Gather information from the group about what is working well and what is not.

From all this, formulate a methodology to use for the balance of the project. If it's early enough in the process, if things are going badly, or if you have time to burn, you may want to evaluate and adopt an existing methodology. However, you may need to content yourself with putting together an *ad hoc* methodology and pushing to completion.

Prevention   Research and evaluate the available OOD methodologies. Don't rely on books, brochures, and salespeople; find groups that have brought projects to completion using a given methodology (or a combination) and quiz them about their experiences. Evaluate a methodology with a small pilot project to see how well it holds up through a complete development cycle. Take note of places where it may become cumbersome or overly complex for a larger project.

Feel free to adapt or combine methodologies. Recognize that some OOD methodologies don't scale well, aren't very easy to use, or may not be well adapted to your problem and solution. But be sure to start development with clear ideas about analysis, design, implementation, and revision; and establish well-defined processes for each phase that yield expected results (documents, diagrams, hierarchies, interfaces, source code, and so on).

Pitfall 3.5: Attempting too much, too soon, too fast.

In some circles, object-oriented development has been touted as dramatically reducing development time. At the same time, promises are made about software reuse, management of complexity, and architectural modularity. Leaving aside the likelihood of achieving such claims, they still inspire or tempt managers and developers alike to leap feet first into object-oriented development, tackling large projects with short deadlines.

The result is like crossing a swamp. The ground starts out a bit damp and the undergrowth a bit thick, but you can make good progress with your OOD machete. As you push ahead, however, you face mud, vines, snakes, water, and alligators in ever-increasing proportions. You may choose to push ahead or to go back, but in either case the effort and cost are greater than if you had used caution before plunging in. And those above you want to know what happened to all the wonderful benefits of OOD.

Symptoms
A project that doesn't seem to be making much progress or one that seems ill-defined.

Consequences
Schedule slips and project failure.

Detection
Enumerate all that you hope to accomplish with this project. See how soon in the process the coding and prototyping started. Measure current status against the announced schedule and make a realistic assessment of where you are.

Extraction
This can be really tough. Once you're in the middle of a project, you have a lot of people counting on you to deliver certain solutions by a particular date. You might be hesitant to stop everything and plan the entire development effort again. On the other hand, there is a good chance—almost a certainty—that if you have stumbled into this pitfall, your efforts to get out of it may not be fully understood or appreciated by those in authority.

Nevertheless, the best solution is to halt development and take the time to scale down the project and train developers; then you can set realistic deadlines.

Prevention
Look again at the pitfall: too much, too soon, too fast. First, start out small when using object-oriented development for the first (or second or third!) time. Use well-defined, small-scale pilot projects.

Or whittle down your large project into a small one on which you can build in later development cycles.

Second, take time for education, analysis, and design. Make sure that everyone involved understands the concepts, techniques, and—yes— the pitfalls of object-oriented development. Resist the temptation to start prototyping and coding immediately; go through an explicit, detailed analysis phase and take time to go through a design phase.

Third, plan for your initial OOD projects to take at least as long as they would if developed using traditional software engineering approaches. You may be pleasantly surprised; you almost certainly won't have a rude awakening. After you get several projects under your belt, you'll become more accurate at projecting development cycles.

Pitfall 3.6: Assuming linear development.

By "linear development," I mean assuming that you can do your software project in a single traditional "waterfall" sequence as defined in Boehm (1976): system requirements, software requirements, preliminary design, detailed design, development and debugging, testing, shipping, maintaining.

This assumption can be risky even using standard structured design methods, but it's dangerous when applied to object-oriented development. It is the nature of object-oriented development to be self-refining. As you push ahead, you suddenly see a new way to factor objects, classes, or even domains. The result is usually a significant reduction in complexity in design and implementation. I've drawn the following graph on whiteboards many times:

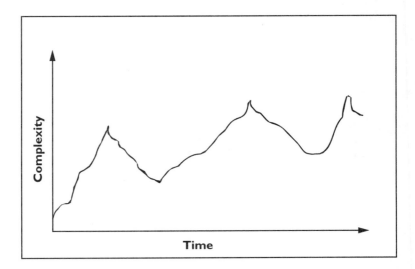

Figure 3.1 Shifts in design and implementation complexity in an object-oriented development effort.

Each of the declines in complexity on the graph represents a period of rethinking, redesign, and changes in implementation. During these periods, implementation of features and functionality comes to a halt; it may even go backward, as working features are thrown out in anticipation of being implemented in a new way. From the outside, these periods are viewed as times of "no progress," making managers and customers nervous. It is often a significant act of faith on their part to believe that real work is being done. You can't even promise that things will be better; in some cases, you need to do this reworking to make the project work at all.

Symptoms Schedules and other project diagrams that show or imply linear development. Constant missing of milestones, especially in the development and testing phases. Heads rolling.

Consequences Projects will be late and deadlines will constantly slip unless the project manager was wise enough to be very generous when scheduling the total time for the project. If milestones are missed, expect panic and finger-pointing.

Detection Look for schedules and other project diagrams that show or imply linear development. Likewise, keep your eyes and ears open for documents and comments indicating an expectation of linear development. For that matter, check your own assumptions.

Extraction Do a hard reset of the project schedule. Make an honest assessment of the project's status; engineers should be brutally honest about the state of the various subsystems. Replan the schedule from the current point, assuming additional periods of decreasing complexity and using a spiral development model (see below).

Prevention First, read the rest of this book and take careful note of all the other pitfalls you might encounter. That may be enough to make you look for another job, but don't despair: If you avoid the pitfalls, you gain the benefits, and you stand a chance of doing things much better and faster.

Second, assume and use a spiral development model, similar to that of Boehm and Papaccio (1988), but with more coding cycles. The idea is to reach an interim level of functionality and then trigger an explicit project review, focusing on complexity, requirements, customer input, and risk assessment. At that point, set new goals for the next cycle—including explicit goals for reduction of complexity—and proceed.

Pitfall 3.7: Allowing the specification to drift or change without agreement.

Let's start by freely acknowledging that, with rare exceptions, software of any complexity changes between original specification and actual delivery. This is to be expected, and to a certain extent encouraged, when the changes represent a refinement of our understanding of the problem domain and the required solutions. Hence Brooks' assertion that we must be prepared to "throw one away"—we just don't know for sure what we'll need to build and how to build it until we've built one. One of the advantages of object-oriented development is that such changes and adaptations can often be made readily and at lower cost in time and risk than for other development approaches.

Let's also acknowledge that, given the time required to deliver a significant piece of software, customer requirements, technical expectations, and market conditions may change dramatically between the time a project is specified and when it is delivered. As John Donovan noted in a recent lecture, the distance between the leading edge of technology and the trailing edge appears to be constantly shrinking. You may need to redirect or revamp projects as they go along in order to respond to such shifts.

But that's not what this pitfall is about. This pitfall is about specifications that aren't nailed down, or that aren't firmly specified at all. A given feature or aspect of the project is discussed (or maybe it isn't). As time goes on, the person(s) implementing it have one idea as to what it means or may even have new and improved ideas for it. Those not implementing it may be assuming something quite different from what is being written. Those not involved—including, and especially, upper management—may have quite a different (and erroneous) idea of what the feature will be. And customer expectations may be something else again. When the time comes for feature completion, code integration, project review, or customer acceptance, all hell breaks loose.

Symptoms   Lack of specification documentation. Engineers showing off "new features." Mismatched subsystems. Constant delays in completing given features.

Consequences Schedule slips due to ever-changing specification and integration problems. Lack of management, marketing, or customer acceptance of the delivered project.

Detection First, see whether you can put your hands on a detailed list of features. If no such list exists or if it is incomplete or vague, then you have problems.

Second, see whether you can find a detailed description for each feature, including clear information about what it will not do. Missing or incomplete information is another danger sign.

Third, compare the specification against what is actually being implemented. Variations are yet another indication of trouble.

Fourth, propose a change in specification and see what is the process for making it. The more informal and undocumented the process, the greater the danger of this pitfall.

Extraction The **Detection** exercise should give you a good idea about your current state and how to get out of it: Produce the documents described and then use them as a hard spec for the project.

A second (not necessarily exclusive) approach is to write a complete user's manual for the project and let that be the final specification. This is what we did at Pages: The user documentation, complete with screen shots, was printed a full nine months before the product was released. The president and CEO of Pages gave a copy to every engineer and said, "Here's the final specification." It saved all of us from the temptation of making further changes.

Prevention Establish a process to create, review, modify, and enforce the specification. This is, in effect, the documentation of the design phase of your methodology. This process won't be easy or popular, but it will pay off significantly in the long run.

Pitfall 3.8: Allowing new features to creep (or pour) in.

The impulse to constantly add new and incremental features to a software program certainly isn't unique to object-oriented development. It derives largely from three sources. Upper management and marketing want, and sometimes need, those additional features to win a customer, to better position the product against a competitor, or to better justify the expense of an in-house project. Engineers often find it far more fun, more interesting, and more rewarding to add or extend features than to make existing features work completely and perfectly. And customers supply a constant flow of demand for new and improved functionality.

The problem is that OOD intensifies all these tendencies. With a decent object-oriented design and implementation, it can take literally only a few minutes to add or extend features. Frankly, that's the payoff that lures many engineers to OOD in the first place: They get to do really neat stuff, do it quickly, and impress the boss while they're at it. The boss, having seen how quickly engineers can extend or create functionality, doubles or trebles the list of must-have features. The technical manager, caught in the middle, wonders how to deal with all this.

Symptoms

Engineers focusing on adding new features instead of getting old ones working completely. Upper management passing down long (or even short) lists of additional features when the engineering schedule will be hard-pressed to accommodate the current ones. Customers failing to distinguish between what they'd like and what they're willing to live with.

Consequences

Features that don't work as completely or well as they were intended. Missed milestones and schedule slippage.

Detection

Review all existing features with the engineering team and get an honest assessment of where each feature is and what it will take to complete it. If necessary, do a design and code review for each feature. Compare the documented "essential features" list—and the schedule required to complete them—with the current feature set as well as those proposed by engineers and upper management, and find where the differences are coming in.

Extraction   Nothing fancy here: Get the absolute "drop dead" release date for the software and work backward from there, allocating time to design, implement, debug, and test each feature that is not yet completed. Show everyone (especially customers) the gap between the time and resources allocated those required for just the currently planned and requested features. Use whatever process works in your company for performing feature triage: keeping those that are absolutely essential, dropping those that can wait for the next release, and negotiating on the others.

Prevention   Use the process given in **Extraction** before a line of code is ever written. As features are proposed, collect them in a list, but do not allow any work on them. At intervals, repeat the process: You might have time (or need) to schedule some of the proposed features, but you may well have to drop previously required ones.

Pitfall 3.9: Mistaking feature prototyping with feature completion.

Object-oriented development often makes it easy for developers to bring up the base functionality for a given feature; to the casual user, it may even appear largely in place. But the gap between what has been done and what needs to be done can be large indeed.

This may be caused by several factors. The developers may genuinely not understand the complete nature of the feature. They may seriously underestimate the work required to complete it. They may not know how to implement the feature as specified. They may find other features more interesting to work on. Or they may be lazy, dishonest, incompetent, or intent on sabotaging the project. This last problem is rare but not unknown.

The greatest danger is that when the missing functionality may not be detected until the project gets close to completion. This not only threatens the schedule for completing that feature but can also have profound ramifications for the entire project. It may turn out to be impossible—or, at least, very difficult—to implement that feature given the design and implementation of the rest of the project. Furthermore, there may be a cascading effect: Other features may not be able to be completed until this one is finished, or the changes required to complete this feature may break other features.

Symptoms   Features that appear *nearly* finished for weeks or even months. Developers who always have a new excuse for not having finished a given feature.

Consequences   Loss or limitation of the feature; schedule slippage to accommodate feature completion; significant redesign and reimplementation of the rest of the project, with major slippage.

Detection   Constant feature review is needed: The current implementation of each feature must be compared against the specification. (There *is* a specification, isn't there?) When a given feature is not making sufficient progress, hold a formal code and design review to see whether there is a serious problem in the approach and intended implementation.

Extraction

On discovering that a given feature is not nearly as comprehensive as you would like, you need to evaluate the situation (as described in **Detection**) and perform triage. If the feature is expendable, drop it. If the complete feature as specified is absolutely essential, then figure out the implications for the rest of the project and for the schedule of pushing through to completion.

If, however, the feature falls between these two extremes, then you enter a process of trading off between feature completeness and schedule slippage. Often, a 70 percent or 80 percent implementation of a feature can be done far more quickly than a 90 percent to 100 percent implementation.

Prevention

For each feature, create a written specification and implementation plan with milestones to completion. Recognize that this document will be modified and expanded as development continues, because both the implementation and the feature itself may change. Use the methods given in **Detection** to keep projects on track.

Pitfall 3.10: Misjudging relative costs.

This is a classic pitfall in software engineering. Typically, insufficient time is allocated for the problem specification, research, design, architecture, and review that should occur before coding and during each development cycle. Likewise, testing is often given little time, money, or people. The whole focus is on coding, and often that is underestimated by assuming that development will be linear (see Pitfall 3.6 and that nothing will go wrong.

Object-oriented development tends to compound this effect in several ways, some of which are discussed elsewhere. First, unrealistic expectations can creep in. Second, rapid prototyping and feature development can cause a false sense of progress. Third, coding may well be genuinely speeded by OOD.

As a result, an expectation can arise that all aspects of the development cycle, not just the coding portion, will be compressed. The first few times you do OOD, it may require more time up front for design and architecture, and it's likely to require as much or more testing time. As your development group gains more experience and expertise in OOD, the entire cycle may start to compress, but that comes with time.

Symptoms
Noncoding tasks taking longer than the time allotted to them. Slowdowns during development due to a need to rethink design. Alpha and beta testing taking much longer than planned.

Consequences
Slipped schedules and missed deadlines. Rude surprises as design must be repeated or testing takes much longer than expected.

Detection
Apply Brooks' rule of thumb: The time required for a project should break down into one-third for design and prototyping, one-sixth for implementing, and half for testing. If your proportions are radically different, then you may have misjudged the relative costs or at least, mislabeled them; a lot of design and testing gets buried inside implementation.

If you're far along in your project, keep a close eye on time required for testing. The time required for testing an object-oriented project can scale geometrically, due to the large number of possible interactions between objects. See Chapter 9, "Quality Assurance Pitfalls," for more details).

Extraction

First, throw out your current schedule and do a hard reset of expectations, particularly among upper management. This is not easy to do, but honesty is always the best policy. Good luck.

Second, set up a development cycle—specify, design, prototype, review, implement, test—with the time allocated to each step in the cycle based roughly on the proportions given above. Recognize that the actual time for each step in each cycle will vary: An early cycle will tend to have more specification and design and less testing; a later cycle will reverse those proportions.

Third, manage through one complete cycle and see how well your estimated costs match reality. Adjust and repeat.

Prevention

First, get some project management software. It doesn't have to be fancy; it just has to automate the task of adding the estimated times for each task, noting critical paths, and calculating a final date. This is important; attempting to schedule anything except the smallest and simplest project in your head will lead to unpleasant surprises.

Second, use steps two and three under **Extraction** to set up your schedule and to estimate relative costs. If possible, try this first with a relatively small project and then work up to larger projects. The goal is to be able to estimate both relative and absolute costs within a certain margin of error (say, 10 percent) on a regular basis.

Pitfall 3.11: Not identifying and managing risks.

What are the risks in object-oriented development? Look at the other 80-plus pitfalls listed in this book to start. Kind of makes you want to take up gardening, doesn't it? On the other hand, being able to identify those risks and then manage them puts you way ahead in the development game and can make you extremely valuable as a technical manager.

Why do we sometimes fail to see and handle risks? There are various reasons. We don't want to confront others and ask hard questions. We don't want to expose our own ignorance. We keep hoping things will correct themselves. We don't want to disappoint or upset those above us. We don't want to have to fire anyone. We don't want to appear not to trust others. We face resistance, forceful or subtle, as we try to point out these risks and deal with them.

Risk management is essential in OOD. It's essential for all the reasons it would be in any software development project. It's essential because the number of engineers who are both skilled and experienced in OOD is still quite small. And it's essential because of the high expectations and mistaken perceptions of nondevelopers concerning OOD. In short, the risks and pitfalls in OOD are greater than those in regular software development—but so are the rewards.

Symptoms   Closed door, closed eyes, closed mind. Constant trickle (or stream) of bad news from developers. Spending more time putting out fires and explaining problems to upper management than actively managing and completing tasks.

Consequences   Slipped schedules, missed milestones, project failures, lost jobs.

Detection   Ask everyone involved with the project what risks they think the project currently faces, with "risks" meaning anything that could cause the project to ship behind schedule, over budget, lacking specified features, in a form not acceptable to customers. If anything comes up you haven't considered and which you aren't handling, then you know you've fallen into this particular pit.

Extraction   Make an exhaustive list detailing all the previously unidentified and unhandled risks that you gleaned from the questioning **Detection**. Distribute the list through the development group and then ask for any additions or corrections (a risk identified by one person may be handled by another). Come up with an assessment of each risk: how probable it is, how it could affect the project, and how it can be managed. Pass this list to upper management. Reset and reschedule the project, if necessary.

Prevention   Risk identification and management should be part of project planning and scheduling from the beginning. The more actively you work as a team to anticipate and handle risks, the fewer problems you'll encounter. Be aware that this takes political courage, though; those above you don't always want to hear what the risks are or why the project may not be completed in the time frame demanded.

Pitfall 3.12: Lying to yourself and others.

Self delusion and group delusion are not uncommon in software development projects. Several factors combine to bring this about. One is the natural optimism prevalent among software engineers, particularly when they are not allowed, encouraged, or required to spend sufficient time specifying and designing what they will develop. Another cause is the presumption that no major roadblocks or difficulties will be encountered along the way, either technical or organizational. A third factor is the not uncommon attitude on the part of upper management that because a project *must* be completed by a certain date, therefore it *can* and *will* be completed by that date, and information to the contrary is not welcome. Mix these and related factors and you have a major disaster in the making.

Again, these tendencies are by no means unique to object-oriented development, but OOD has a way of magnifying them. Engineers become even more optimistic, technical managers see fewer roadblocks, and upper management, having read all the glowing articles about OOD in the business and trade publications, expects unrealistic results.

Symptoms   Irritation, anger, and disbelief when someone gives unpopular but honest appraisals of how things are going. Long, earnest explanations of why the standard rules of software development don't apply in this case. And, of course, serious discrepancies between the planned schedule and actual results.

Consequences   Constant slips in the schedule, as expectations are continually reset to adjust to the new version of reality. Projects that ship very late, if at all. Loss of credibility for managers and developers.

Detection   Take aside the developers, managers, and others involved in the project, one at a time, and ask each person, "Do you think there's anything we're fooling ourselves about?" Make notes of the points each person brings up. Make a second pass through, but this time show them the list you've compiled and ask them what they agree with, what they disagree with, and what they'd like to add. The number and significance of items on the list should give you a good idea whether you and others are fooling yourselves about how the project is going.

Extraction Given a significant list of items, you need to reschedule and plan again based on the information collected. This may not be easy or popular; in some cases, it may not even be possible, depending on how upper management reacts. Your choice may then be to either push ahead as best you can or find another job.

Prevention Use the process described under **Detection** from the start of project planning and design. You may sacrifice popularity, but you'll gain credibility—provided, of course, that they don't reassign (or fire) you and put someone more amenable in charge.

Pitfall 3.13: Using the wrong metrics.

That which gets measured gets accomplished—or, at least, evaluated. That's why various software metrics are used as an indication of progress and accomplishment. The best known—and easiest to compute—is lines of code (LOC), usually measured as thousands of lines of code (KLOC). Luckily, LOC is slowly losing its appeal, because it encourages verbosity and constant additions to the code base, even though simplicity and refinement of existing code are ideal. Function points (FPs) are trendier, but they're also harder to measure and so don't get used as often.

The point is that these metrics and many others have little bearing on object-oriented development.

Use of the "wrong" metrics is probably better than no metrics at all. In one project I worked on, we tracked the change in LOC on a subproject basis week by week; it gave a rough indication of activity in and stability of a subproject.

Symptoms   Use of metrics that don't appear to be meaningful or that, worse yet, are misleading.

Consequences   Time is spent generating information that is of little value and that may give a misleading or erroneous indication of how the project is progressing. More seriously, developers may be encouraged, consciously or unconsciously, to "produce" in ways that run counter to the goals of the project.

Detection   Find out which metrics are being used (if any). Consider their influence and impact; see whether they help predict time or quality of development. Ask other people how they interpret these metrics.

Extraction   Abandon all irrelevant metrics and adopt appropriate ones. Educate all parties involved about what is being done and why. Establish benefits and rewards for those who take the time to use the metrics and whose development efforts improve as a result.

Prevention   From the outset, educate everyone—developers, technical managers, upper management—about what are the appropriate metrics and what they mean. Develop tools to automate metric generation as much as possible. Use the metrics regularly; distribute the results and discuss their meaning.

Several articles and at least one book (Lorenz and Kidd) discuss appropriate metrics for object-oriented development. Here are a few of the proposed metrics for OOD:

- time for analysis, design, implementation, testing
- average worker-days per class, average number of classes per developer
- rate of change of class and subsystem interface
- hierarchy metrics, including nesting level, number of abstract classes, "fanout" (number of derived classes per base class)

  class metrics (both average and per class), including number of class variables, number of instance variables, number of class methods, number of instance methods, and number of overridden methods
- instance metrics, including size (in bytes) per instance, number of instances during execution, and number of persistent instances
- method metrics, including size (in lines of code), number of parameters
- coupling and cohesion metrics, including number of classes referenced by a given class
- reuse metrics, including number of classes used in more than one project

Be sure to automate these metrics as much as possible; trying to do these by hand will work once or twice but will not give you the constant feedback you need to make them truly useful. Case in point: Do you think anyone would use or continue to use the old "lines of code" metric if they had to count them by hand?

Pitfall 3.14: Using the wrong developers.

Various industry studies cite the productivity gap between the best and the worst developers. Awhile there is some controversy over the ranges often cited (such as the famous 26:1 figure), anyone who has managed a diverse group of developers won't argue with the fact that there can be a dramatic difference in productivity among individuals.

What is less obvious is that given a group of developers who are roughly equal in having a sufficient or even superior level of competence and productivity, not all of them will readily adapt to object-oriented architecture, design and implementation. Some developers will take to it quickly and do very well; others will have to work harder, but will eventually come up to speed; yet others may never become skilled in OOD even though they may not be aware of this fact.

When this happens, all the developers may be working hard, but the relative quality of their work—measured by adherence to good OO principles—can vary dramatically. This may not be apparent for some time, and when it does appear, it can be difficult to correct, from both a technical and organizational viewpoint.

Symptoms   Product architecture that must constantly be revised or refactored. Subsystems that are less stable than others or that are hard to integrate with the rest of the project. Developers consistently complaining about the quality or utility of a given developer's code.

Consequences Varying quality within the product; reduction of classic OO benefits; friction and even serious rifts between team members; project or product failure.

Detection   It's a big help to have someone who you know is skilled at OOD. That can be harder to determine than you think, even (or especially) if you think that *you're* skilled at OOD. If the symptoms appear, then a code and design review for that person's subsystems would be the appropriate first step. At the same time, a means of evaluating the developer's OO skills will provide a cross-check.

Extraction   This can be one of the hardest issues for a manager, especially if the developer doesn't recognize the deficiencies. The best solution is probably one of obvious or subtle mentoring: partnering that developer with someone of proven OO skills. This approach has two aims: to get the project back on track and to bring the developer's skills up to speed.

Prevention   Seek the best developers. That may sound obvious, but a lot of companies are more interested in head count than talent and adaptability. The developer should be a self-starter and keenly interested in OOD, and should also have professional software engineering skills and the discipline to match.

Before the project even starts, spend time to train the developers, and promote the explicit understanding that their OO skills will be evaluated on a regular basis. Provide incentives for honesty and alternative assignments, such as building tools, for those whose skills lie elsewhere.

Conclusion

Much has been said so far about the need to train and educate developers for object-oriented development. There is an equal—perhaps an even greater—need to train and educate technical managers, both in object-oriented development and in how to manage OOD projects.

To be a successful manager of OOD projects, you must be able and willing to do these three things:

- correctly set and manage the expectations of upper management
- correctly evaluate the skills and progress of your individual developers
- correctly judge the current state of the project and the required time to completion

That's a piece of cake, right? All it takes is a lot of studying, a lot of practice, and a lot of experience. Several books and other resources to help you with your studying are listed in the Bibliography; the rest is up to you and your team.

References

Boehm, Barry W. "Software engineering," *IEEE Transactions on Computers*. C-25(12), December 1976.

Boehm, Barry W. and Philip N. Papaccio, "Understanding and controlling software costs," *IEEE Transactions on Software Engineering*. 4(10), October 1988.

Booch, Grady. "The Booch method: process and pragmatics" in Carmichael, Andy (ed.), *Object Development Methods*. New York: SIGS Books, 1994.

Brooks, Frederick P., Jr. *The Mythical Man-Month*. Reading, Mass: Addison-Wesley, 1979.

Lorenz, Mark and Jeff Kidd, *Object-Oriented Software Metrics*. Englewood Cliffs, N.J.: Prentice Hall, 1994.

Parkhill, Dave. "Object-oriented technology transfer: techniques and guidelines for a smooth transition," *Object Magazine*. 2(1), May/June 1992.

CHAPTER 4:

ANALYSIS AND DESIGN PITFALLS

I cannot imagine any condition which would cause a ship to founder....Modern shipbuilding has gone beyond that.

— Capt. Edward J. Smith, six years before commanding the *Titanic* on its maiden voyage

Traditional analysis and design efforts in software engineering tend to focus on one of four aspects: the actions being carried out (process-oriented analysis or functional decomposition); the information being manipulated (data-flow analysis); the various program states (state-flow analysis); or the events to be handled.

Object-oriented analysis and design goes a long way toward bringing all four aspects together. Because objects contain information and the actions that work on it, you end up addressing the problem in terms of process and data simultaneously. State modeling can be done in terms of states of each object, and events map nicely onto messages and methods.

But that doesn't make OOAD obvious or simple, even—or especially—given strong skills in traditional methods. We often carry into our current efforts a bias towards our previous approaches. We may flounder a bit until we've been through the process a few times and start to get good at it.

Analysis and design pitfalls can come from the struggle to manage complexity while gaining a sense of how object technology really works. If you're new at this—and probably even if you aren't—just assume that you're going to go through two or three major exercises in rearchitecting as you learn how to map your design to the problem domain.

This chapter is geared largely toward technical managers and architects, though it can be of great use to developers as a self-check.

Pitfall 4.1: Underestimating the need for analysis and design.

Bosses and customers like results. They like a development effort that takes less time and money then they fear it will take, which is why they agreed to (or dictated) the use of object-oriented development in the first place. And they want to see results as soon as possible—tangible results that show up on a computer screen and appear to be *doing* something. Sometimes they are unimpressed with specification documents and diagrams; they equate paperwork with busywork and bureaucracy, not with creation, genius, and careful thought. Occasionally, deep (or not so deep) in their hearts and minds lurks the suspicion that developers are spoiled, lazy, and looking for ways to avoid doing real work, so bosses and customers want proof of actual coding progress.

Engineers like results, too. They like to plunge their hands into the primordial bit-ooze and make things. Show a software engineer a problem and he may be already thinking of a half dozen ways to solve it before you're through explaining the issues, and he'll be itching to get in and start working on it *right now*. For some engineers, the prospect of spending days, weeks, or months doing analysis and design can be agonizing.

When these two forces meet and reinforce each other, analysis and design scarcely stand a chance. The focus is to plunge into implementation immediately and push ahead, making course corrections as problems arise. The irony is that the analysis and design will end up being done anyway, but piecemeal as the project reacts to crises and issues.

Symptoms Few resources (time, people) devoted to analysis and design in the development schedule; skepticism and hostility toward analysis and design on the part of upper management, technical managers, and developers.

Consequences The project will take longer, cost more, be less suited to the customer, and result in a lower return on investment (in terms of reuse gains and revision costs) than if the analysis and design had been done up front.

Detection If a project hasn't started, ask yourself and others (above and below) this question: How much time should we plan on devoting to analysis and design? Any answers of less than 25 percent of a given development cycle (analysis, design, implementation, testing) are a serious warning that you are near or in the pitfall.

If the project is already under way, note how much time was actually spent as well as any resistance that has occurred from individuals and groups at all levels. Also observe shifts in design and implementation that have occurred because of insufficient analysis and design.

Extraction   In this situation, extraction may be easier than prevention, though for an unpleasant reason: because the project isn't going well. On the other hand, it may still be difficult to do what needs to be done, which is to suspend or dramatically slow development while revisiting analysis and design.

Prevention   First, set up a development schedule in which 25 percent to 35 percent of the time involved is devoted to analysis and design. As noted in **Extraction,** this can be tough if you lack evidence of actual problems to convince those who underestimate the need. This is where starting with a pilot project (low cost, low risk) can be a large help: It gives you a chance to demonstrate the benefits of doing a proper job of analysis and design. The 25 to 35 percent figure might be smaller for a revision of an existing project, but not substantially so; in fact, in project revisions the temptation is often strongest to push into implementation without thinking through what really should be done.

Second, get the engineers excited about the creative aspects of analysis and design. This is no mean feat, but it can be done first by securing the support of the leaders (*de facto* if not *de jure*) in the engineering team; second, by making it a matter of team pride; and third, by introducing competition and group expectations. (See writings by De Marco and Lister in the References section for details on engineering team building.)

Third, be persistent and hard-nosed about making sure that the analysis and design are thorough and complete.

Pitfall 4.2: Underestimating the difficulty of analysis and design.

Analysis and design are tough, especially when they're done well and thoroughly. Listed below are some of the steps that can be involved, compiled from the various object methodologies.

Analysis consists of identifying and defining the following:

- the problem domain
- user requirements and needs
- the methodology to be used, including object model and notation
- classes from the problem domain
- subjects in the problem domain
- object responsibilities
- class hierarchies
- object structures (whole and part)
- class and instance attributes
- class and instance methods
- object relationships and interactions
- state transitions
- information locations, including persistent information and data dictionaries
- event flows and message sequences
- dynamic models, including use cases and scenarios

Design consists of specifying the following:

- class and object internals
- abstract vs. concrete classes
- data management, including instance ownership and persistence
- user interface and interactions with the system
- subsystems and modules, including interfaces and cohesion and coupling

There is substantial disagreement about the boundary between analysis and design, which items go where, or even which items are necessary. Regardless of how you manipulate the list above, you still need to carry out most of these tasks, and they aren't easy.

Symptoms   Lack of concern about the resources and effort required for analysis and design. Lack of support for investing the required resources and effort. Constant or intermittent *ad hoc* efforts at analysis and design.

Consequences   Major schedule slips. Products that are poorly designed or that don't sufficiently address the customers' needs.

Detection   Compare the above checklists with your concept of analysis and design. Now compare them with the concepts and expectations of others. Now imagine what it will take to do all these tasks.

Extraction   Use the checklists to identify what has and hasn't been done in the project so far. Sit down with all involved to review the lists and plan the additional work that needs to be done.

Prevention   Use the process in **Detection** and **Extraction** to raise everyone's awareness of what must be done.

Pitfall 4.3: Pouring new wine into old bottles (or vice versa).

The Biblical parable that cautioned against this practice referred to the danger of new wine fermenting and causing the old leather wineskins to split open. The meaning of the parable is that to attempt to fit a new approach or set of rules into an old way of doing things can damage both and cause your efforts to be lost.

The pitfall here is to attempt to use object-oriented techniques in the context of classic analysis and design. This is a natural tendency: We want to focus on what is familiar and what we do well. If we're new to OOD, we're not going to necessarily think in "object" terms. Instead, we're going to approach the problem the way we know best.

Two possible situations are identified in this pitfall. First, you may take a classic approach to analysis and design and then attempt to implement it using object-oriented techniques. Second, you may attempt an object-oriented analysis and design but then create your classes, with their hierarchies and connections, more along the lines of traditional programs. In both cases, you'll often get objects that tend to look either like slightly intelligent data structures or like procedural libraries (Pitfall 7.6), and there may be a lot of confusion about relationships between object classes (Pitfall 7.1).

Symptoms Difficulties in setting up class hierarchies; misshapen or illogical hierarchies. Classes that look a lot like libraries or data structures. Poor mapping between object classes and problem domains. Poor class design, including relationships between classes.

Consequences Poor solution to problems. Loss of benefits from OOD; disillusionment with OOD. Project slip and all that entails.

Detection Read books on object-oriented analysis and design (see the references at the end of this chapter) and then take another look at your project. Focus on how well object classes map to the problem domain.

Extraction This depends in part on how far you are into analysis, design, or development when you become aware of the problem. If the project is far advanced and can be completed as designed, then you should probably push ahead to the end and just do better the next time. If it's early in the process or if the project is in danger of getting seriously stuck, then you may need to reset and rethink your whole design.

Prevention Before you start the project, decide whether to use object-oriented development. Go back and read Chapter 1 to ensure that you're adopting OOD for the right reasons and have a good understanding of the risks involved.

If you are going to push ahead with OOD, you and other affected people should study object-oriented analysis and design. Proceed slowly at first, and look for ways to simplify and generalize; good object-oriented designs tend to resolve to general principles. Use small pilot projects when possible to practice and test the principles you're learning. Have those who gain experience this way act as mentors and instructors to others in the group.

Pitfall 4.4: Not being aware of your blind spots.

Software development is fraught with risks in part because of the difficulty of completely specifying the desired solution ahead of time. Even when both the need and the difficulty of analysis and design are recognized and accepted, the effort may fall short. There are many reasons this may happen; here are three:

Not knowing what you don't know. This is the ultimate challenge in any human endeavor: dealing with the scope of our ignorance. Although we can mark the boundaries between knowledge and ignorance, we cannot, with complete assurance, identify all that lies beyond. Unfortunately, too often we don't even try. Analysis is as important for learning what we don't know as what we do know, because we can then seek to classify our ignorance and decompose it into smaller, bounded, manageable chunks.

Classifying only what you observe. A key part of every object-oriented analysis methodology is to identify object classes. There is a danger, because of haste, pressure, or laziness, to limit our analysis and classification to that which we observe. By so doing, we ignore or remain blind to those aspects of the problem domain that are not readily observable, such as manual operations; physical repositories; and unspoken assumptions or unobserved realities of technique, process, and politics.

Ignoring subjects and focusing only on objects. Because we are dealing with object-oriented development, we sometimes neglect the subjects that act upon objects: users, systems, and other objects. The results of our analysis and design may have too much object orientation and not enough subject orientation.

Symptoms   Incomplete analysis and design showing up through the need for constant revisions and additions to the project.

Consequences   Schedule slip; frequent updates to the specification; possibly even project failure.

Detection   Hold sessions with all those involved in the project: customers, upper management, and developers. Ask them, "What have we overlooked or failed to consider? What don't we know enough (or anything) about? Where are the greatest risks in our design and implementation?" If you're not comfortable with the quality of the answers, then bring in some outside consultants and have them seek answers to the same questions.

Extraction   Use the results from **Detection** to revisit the analysis and design efforts. You may need to halt implementation for a while until you are convinced that you have a sufficiently complete design to push ahead.

Prevention   Use the **Detection** and **Extraction** process at the start of analysis; repeat it regularly. The more you probe the boundaries of your ignorance, the more likely they are to shrink. It's a good idea to bring in a fresh point of view from time to time to avoid falling into a rut.

Pitfall 4.5: Building a too-general or too-complete solution.

Normally, a general or complete solution is not a Bad Thing; in fact, it's often a Very Good Thing. Generality usually makes code more flexible; it often makes the code more powerful; and it leads to greater code reuse. Because object-oriented development focuses on abstraction, it leads us to generalize abstract classes and then instantiate concrete subclasses.

All this sounds wonderful. How can it be a pitfall?

Simple: It's a pitfall when you get so caught up in the effort to make your solution general or complete that you lose sight of the constraints of the original problem. Suppose your mandate is to write a simple custom database browser to be delivered in one month. If you try to write a full-blown graphical database front end, only to find month after month slipping by, you have failed in your assignment and have damaged your company, no matter how wonderful your more general solution is. Furthermore, an attempt to make things too general or complete too soon can leave you floundering or drifting down wrong alleys, because you don't yet have a full grasp of the problem. You may never come up with a general or complete solution, and the project may die as a result.

Symptoms
Programs that are getting too big, too slow, or too difficult for users. Architects or engineers who talk about wanting to do a more general solution. Subsystems that seem to take forever to be completed.

Consequences
Missed milestones; projects that are late or that never ship; programs that do more than customers want or care about. See also Pitfalls 2.6, 3.5, 3.7, and 3.8.

Detection
This pitfall is hard to detect, because—as noted above—generality and completeness are usually virtues in an object-oriented design. Sometimes it is far better to have a project slip for the sake of a more general approach, because it will pay off later when you need to fix or extend the program. It may also give the users a solution far superior to the one originally requested.

It boils down to two questions. First, what return will you get on the investment of extra time and effort? Each month—each day—a project is late equates with a loss of revenue and opportunity. If the generalization is critical for acceptance and success, then you should spend the time. Likewise, you may need the generalization to avoid creating significant problems for yourself later. If, on the other hand, the users don't care, you'll be hard pressed to justify the extra time.

Second, what opportunities will there be to generalize later? If you're doing a custom in-house application, you may be better off delivering a more limited and specific version and then applying user feedback to see what generalizations will improve a subsequent version.

Extraction   This can be hard, depending on the state of things when you detect this pitfall. If you catch the move toward generalization just as it begins, then you can do the analysis discussed above and make a decision based on it. If, however, significant effort has been put into it before it's caught, you may be in a dilemma: whether to shut down the effort and try for a simpler implementation or to go ahead and push it to completion. At that point, it's up to your best judgment—and that's what experience is for.

Prevention   We have a saying in the Pages engineering group: "Start out stupid and work up from there." Even when you want a general or complete solution, it is often best to implement it using an iterative design-and-code cycle, starting out with a bare-bones approach, verifying its behavior and functionality, and then working up to the next level. This approach has three important benefits. First, you can set up your development to take things in smaller, more easily managed and predictable chunks. Second, if you hit a conceptual roadblock, or begin to suffer under time constraints, you have a working subsystem at some level of functionality. Third, you can more quickly test and detect whether you're going in the right direction, allowing you to change direction with less backtracking and less time lost.

Pitfall 4.6: Having the wrong number of architects.

Because of the process-plus-data nature of objects, it is often easy to divide an object-oriented development project into several domains or subsystems and then parcel them out to different developers. Each developer designs a subsystem, defines the interface that the subsystem presents to the others, and then proceeds with the implementation. Other developers who want to use that subsystem just learn the interface and follow it; the implementation is hidden (the term, remember, is *encapsulated*) behind the interface and can be modified without concern. It sounds wonderfully modular, egalitarian, and object-oriented.

Unfortunately, it's also a recipe for disaster. Having a chief architect, possibly heading a small architectural team, is absolutely critical on an object-oriented development project of any size. Why? Because the "interface" for a given subsystem or even a given class is far more than just the syntax of the C++ class declarations, the Objective-C interface section, or the equivalent in whatever language you're using. There are numerous assumptions of semantics and intent, too often undocumented, about how and when methods are to be used, the pre- and post conditions for each method, the set of allowable states for object instances or even classes, the ownership of object components, and the obvious or subtle relationships and connections between objects. Furthermore, you need an independent check on how well a given subsystem has been implemented and whether it meets the needs and intentions of the overall project.

Without a chief architect to shape those semantics and intentions, you can have subsystems or classes that appear to talk with one another but make fundamentally wrong or misguided assumptions about one another. You can lose much time as developers learn the idiosyncrasies of each subsystem or class, seeing no common approach or metaphor. You can fall into many of the other pitfalls listed in this book as developers patch and extend subsystems and classes, theirs or those of others, to make things work.

Beyond that, there is a higher probability of having a coherent, unified design and architecture when there is a chief architect, even if this person heads a small architectural team. It doesn't mean that no one else can contribute to design; it just means that one person (the right person, one hopes) needs to receive all input and fit what's appropriate into the architecture.

Symptoms   Fragile architecture; difficulties in coordination between subsystems and classes; differences in assumptions, theme, or approach between subsystems and classes; ego clashes among developers.

Consequences   High incidence of bugs; low reliability; tardiness in shipping; difficulties in extending or fixing the application.

Detection   First-order detection: Ask yourself, "Who's the chief architect for this project?" If you can't answer that yourself, then you have problems.

Second-order detection: Gather the development team and ask, "Who's the chief architect for this project?" If there's any disagreement, grumbling, or flaring egos, then you have a problem.

Third-order detection: If you ask the chief architect, "What is your plan for maintaining architectural unity in this project?" and you don't get a simple, coherent answer, you have problems.

Extraction   There are two social problems: picking a chief architect and getting everyone else to accept him or her (which includes recognizing the chief's authority to tell them to do things differently). This is hard to do for a project in progress, and there may be subtle and blatant ego flares at this; think of lizards inflating their dewlaps and baring their teeth.

Having solved that problem, you face at least one major technical problem: cleaning things up. This may not be easy; it may not even be possible, beyond some general rationalizing of the interfaces, if the project is too far along. At least you're laying the groundwork for future efforts.

Prevention   Brooks argues far more eloquently than I can about the need for a chief architect in any software project. He also discusses at length the various social and ego implications of architects vs. contractors. I won't repeat his arguments here; you can read what he has to say. But recognize this: Implementation is generally more challenging and more interesting than design and architecture.

Pitfall 4.7: Making things too complex.

Generally speaking, undue complexity in an object-oriented system is a danger signal. Excess complexity within a class may indicate that the class does not map well to the problem domain, though this is the level at which complexity may well exist and be encapsulated.

Excess complexity in a class interface may indicate that the class is too large, that it's attempting too much, or that it's poorly designed. A complex interface makes it difficult for someone to use the class; it also obscures even more the semantic interface of the class—information you need to understand about the class that isn't stated in the interface source code.

Excess complexity within a class hierarchy suggests the need for some rethinking or refactoring. Excess complexity between classes or subsystems may indicate that there is poor encapsulation, high coupling, or poor system design.

Object-oriented development makes it easy to make things complex. You can readily create new classes, rearrange hierarchies, add data and function members to objects, construct new objects from old ones, have objects talk to each other, and so on. In fact, it's easy to do all this and still have everything compile and (usually) run.

OOD also makes it easy to push rapidly forward into a degree of complexity from which you may not be able to back out with equal ease. If you don't have a good system of source code control, you may not be able to back out at all.

Symptoms   Many of the pitfalls mentioned in Chapter 7, "Class and Object Pitfalls", are symptomatic of an object-oriented design that is too complex. Beyond that, when you have trouble tracking flow of control (especially during debugging) or explaining the principles that underlie the design, things have gotten too complex. Also note **Consequences**, below.

Consequences   Unpredictability of program or subsystem behavior. Too many bugs, many of which are difficult to track down. Poor performance. Program fails to behave consistently. Difficulty using classes and subsystems, fixing bugs, or adding features.

Detection   When symptoms show up, hold appropriate code and design reviews to verify that things are too complex; recognize that some solutions are by nature complex and may not be able to be further decomposed and rationalized. Preemptively, ask architects and developers to identify systems they believe are too complex or are heading in that direction.

Extraction If things are getting too complex, spend time talking and thinking about how to simplify and clarify the design and implementation. Then judge whether you can afford the time and effort to do so, and act accordingly.

Prevention Good, solid thought and discussion before coding begins will do wonders to reduce or manage growth of complexity as the project goes along. Appoint and empower a good chief architect (see Pitfall 4.6). Establish methods to detect complexity and procedures to deal with it.

Pitfall 4.8: Designing by enumeration.

Design by enumeration is what it says: listing all possible states, cases, or situations that a given object or object system can be in and then basing domain, class, and object design on that enumeration without first abstracting a general design. This tends to lead to poor design for several reasons.

First, you are bound to overlook possible states in all but the simplest of systems. You may be hard-pressed to identify all possible states; if you consider all factors defining a given state, you may find it impossible to enumerate all states—there may be far too many.

Second, the resulting domain, class, or object design tends to focus on detecting a given state and handling it. As new states are identified, more state-specific code is added. This tends to make systems and objects very complex very quickly (see Pitfall 4.7).

Third, the resulting objects and systems tend to be inflexible, hard to reuse or extend, easily broken, and difficult to fix. They usually have lots of special-case code that tests for and handles explicit conditions.

Symptoms Subsystems and classes that take much longer to implement than expected, must be constantly patched and revised to handle new cases, and are much harder to debug or modify than usual.

Consequences Incomplete subsystems, missed milestones, and delayed projects.

Detection Some architects or developers will come out and tell you that they're doing design by enumeration, which is a good clue. Short of that, pay attention when you have a developer coming back repeatedly to tell you of a given class or subsystem, "It wasn't handling *some specific case*, but I fixed it." That isn't a definite indicator, but it's a clue. Ask the developer whether code was put in just to handle that case or whether an adjustment was made to a more general solution.

Extraction As with other situations, it depends on how far along you are and the chances of making things work as they stand. If you're far along, under time pressure, and can make things work, then push ahead and rearchitect for the next version of the program. If you can't wait, then you'll have to rearchitect now.

Prevention Design by abstraction. Start with enumeration and then look for trends, patterns, and general categories. Ponder the essence of the thing being represented by the class or subsystem and its "natural" attributes and behaviors. As the design begins to coalesce, run it through whatever additional enumerations you or others can think of; if some situations are not handled, then go back and think more about the abstraction.

Pitfall 4.9: Rearchitecting too often or for the wrong reasons.

One of the exhilarating aspects of object-oriented development for developers is the low cost—apparent or real—of rearchitecting a subsystem or even the entire project. Dramatic changes to internal implementations, reorganization and rationalization of interfaces, and new organizations of cooperating objects can often be done rapidly. This can be a tremendous benefit when you hit a roadblock or when you come across a significantly superior way of doing things.

Unfortunately, it can also lure architects and developers into rearchitecting for less than compelling reasons: in pursuit of unnecessary generalization or refinement, out of intellectual curiosity or challenge, to alleviate boredom, to show off, or just because it can be done. Sometimes a new architecture is started before the current architecture has been developed enough to see whether it will work.

Symptoms   Subsystems or classes in a frequent or constant state of flux.

Consequences   Never getting the project sufficiently stable or functional to evaluate it, resulting in it's being late or canceled. Subsystems that do something other than what is desired.

Detection   First, you have to be able to detect whether a subsystem or class is being rearchitected. This isn't necessarily easy; when developers start rearchitecting, they often get quiet, set out a smokescreen, and keep to themselves a lot, preferring to present their efforts as a *fait accompli*. They know that it's easier to ask forgiveness than permission; a lot of excellent and even vital engineering gets done this way, and technical managers usually develop a sense of when to allow it and when to rein it in.

Second, you have to decide whether the rearchitecting is happening too often or for the wrong reasons. Determining frequency is relatively easy: How many times has this happened in a given period of time, and how long has it been since the last architecture? Determining the reason can be trickier, especially if you're not in a position, for technical or other reasons, to evaluate both the previous architecture and the targeted one. You may need help from other architects and developers, but be prepared for some turf wars.

Extraction   If it's happening, you need to apply the brakes. If possible, roll back to the previous revision; in any case, require that a formal review be done of both the current and the proposed architectures. Use that as a basis for deciding what changes, if any, should be made to the architecture of the given class or subsystem. And, of course, make sure that rearchitecture happens when it is really needed; see Pitfall 4.10.

Prevention The first-order solution is to have a chief architect who oversees all implementations and who must approve any rearchitecting. If the chief architect is responsible for the excess, you'll need to institute a review process and also educate the chief architect about the realities of software development—namely, the need to ship products on schedule.

Pitfall 4.10: Rearchitecting too seldom.

You may remember this diagram from Chapter 3:

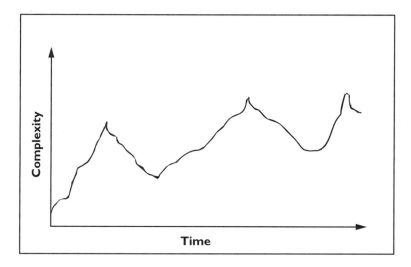

Figure 4.1 Shifts in design and implementation complexity in an object-oriented development effort.

This shows the normal trend in object-oriented development projects. As a certain level of complexity is reached, new ways appear of defining, arranging, and relating classes and subsystems, leading to a reduction in complexity and often to greater generality in the implementation.

Without this periodic reassessment and rearchitecting, project complexity increases continually over time. In a perfectly designed, architected, and implemented project, that would not necessarily be wrong; just draw a straight line between the end-points of the line in the above graph, and you end up at the same spot.

Such a path, however, is rare in all but very simple projects or in those that are very well defined and in a domain in which you are highly experienced. For most of us mortals, object-oriented development is a process of discovery and refinement. If we fail to allow the time to use what we've learned and clean up our architecture, we risk never delivering our project.

Symptoms   Increasing complexity and fragility of application; difficulty in adding new features.

Consequences   A fragile, buggy, possibly late application that is hard to modify and hard to fix.

Detection   The biggest clue is presence of a class or subsystem that gets increasingly bloated, obscure, unstable, and difficult to debug and extend. To catch this, you have three nonexclusive alternatives:

- If you're technically able, you can review source code for possible problem areas.
- Ask developers whether there are areas that they believe should not be rearchitected; they will often be quite frank, especially if it's not their own code.
- Hold design and code reviews on a regular or as-needed basis.

Extraction   Once you've found a subsystem or class that needs to be rearchitected, evaluate what work must be done, its costs and risks, and who can best do it. Then decide whether you can afford to do it and whether you can afford *not* to do it. These answers are not mutually exclusive. If you can afford only one path, then that's your decision. If you can afford both paths, then it becomes your judgment call, based on long-term implications. If you can't afford either path, then you have far bigger problems than just rearchitecting a given subsystem.

Prevention   Before the project starts, discuss the possible need for periodic rearchitecting of subsystems and schedule the appropriate time based on your best estimates. Adopt an iterative design/implementation cycle that allows windows for architecture review and revamping. Establish a process to trigger and conduct reviews. Give the chief architect the responsibility and authority for keeping abreast of all subsystem and class architectures.

Pitfall 4.11: Pleasing the wrong audience.

Software products have a tendency toward "feature drift." It represents a growing gap between how a feature is supposed to work—or how users would like it to work—and how it is implemented. That's because developers tend to develop the product to please themselves and those to whom they report.

There are several reasons for this. Those involved in a development project often may not actually perform the tasks for which the finished software application is intended. Even if they would actually use the application, developers often have a different approach and workflow process than the target users, especially if the intended users don't have a strong computer background. Engineers spend so much time using the software under development that what becomes obvious to them often remains obscure for users. And engineers are not above implementing a given feature in a certain way because it's easier to do so.

The twist is that object-oriented development often suggests new and different approaches to tasks. An engineer might implement a given feature a certain way because the object-oriented approach favors that method or because a more traditional approach might be more difficult in the context of the object architecture and implementation.

The flip side is that the new approach may actually be favored by users. But without the proper research and cross-checks, there's no way of being sure of that.

Symptoms   Engineers modifying features to work differently "because it's a lot easier to implement this way" or "this really reflects the architecture more." Note that the second reason may be valid, but if the result doesn't please the intended customers it doesn't matter.

Consequences   A product that is not readily accepted by its intended audience and that has high training and support costs.

Detection   Have actual target users sit down and use the product, focusing on any features that you might be particularly concerned about. See whether the users can figure out how to use the product and its features with a minimum of help or training. Get their feedback on how they want things to work.

Extraction   When this happens in mid-project, you need to perform triage on the implementation of each feature in question. If the feature can be changed to suit the users without much impact, then do so. If changing the feature implementation would have an unacceptable impact on the schedule (and possibly on other features), then leave it alone and wait for the next version to modify that particular feature. If things are somewhere in-between, then figure out how to make the feature more acceptable at the minimal cost to your schedule and resources.

Prevention   Involve users from the very beginning. Do lots of testing to see what they like and what they don't like. If you have grand new ideas, try them out on the users via prototypes. As development proceeds, have periodic reality checks as noted in **Detection**.

Pitfall 4.12: Forcing a new paradigm on users.

Use of object-oriented analysis and design techniques can lead to new approaches to solving existing problems. These new approaches are sometimes more intuitive than old ones, and they are usually more powerful. But if the resulting application compels the user to understand and adopt a new work paradigm, be prepared for unpleasant results.

Once computer users know how to accomplish a task a given way, they will often be quite resistant to having to adopt a new solution. This is not necessarily due to intellectual inflexibility but is rooted instead in the myriad of conscious and unconscious patterns and reflexes that build up when performing a task repeatedly. We are creatures of habit.

For example, suppose you could prove that it was far superior to control a car by steering with the feet (via pedals) and controlling acceleration and braking using a joystick. Now suppose that every car in a given city were transformed overnight to this new approach (much like swapping applications on a network server). Just imagine what traffic would be like the next morning, how many accidents would occur, and how long it would be (if ever) before traffic flowed as smoothly as it had before the changeover.

This example may seem contrived, but we do the same thing by mandating paradigm shifts for our customers. A paradigm shift is not bad in and of itself, but it must reflect the users' needs and expectations.

Symptoms   Slow acceptance by customers. Drop in productivity by adopters. Long lists of complaints by users. Files and other forms of data being incomplete or getting lost.

Consequences   If your product is commercial, it may fail in the marketplace. If it's a custom app for internal deployment, it may trigger political and business struggles over deployment; even if it's adopted, your company may lose productivity. In any case, your job may be at risk.

Detection   Conduct usability studies. Invite potential customers to use the product, offering only a minimum of instruction or explanation. Note where they get stuck and what they don't understand.

Videotape them trying to use the product. Ask them afterward what they expected, what they felt was missing, and what confused them.

Extraction

This is both simple and tough: Rewrite the application to better suit the expectations and work patterns of your users. You may face significant internal resistance to doing so. But the best and most effective way to overcome both problems is to do usability testing with current or potential customers. This will give you the best feedback and will help you overcome internal resistance to the necessary changes.

Note in your testing, however, this piece of hard-bought wisdom from Larry Spelhaug, Pages' president and CEO: "Don't confuse what beta testers tell you with what actual customers want to buy."

Prevention

Customer research. Customer feedback. Customer use. Note that this pitfall says nothing about new paradigms being bad *perse*; it is when you force users to adopt a new paradigm that they don't want or need—and that doesn't convey a compelling benefit—that problems arise.

Conclusion

The skill of object-oriented programming—much less object-oriented analysis and design—cannot be acquired overnight. We bring our past with us, and some things we must unlearn. Books will help, and the books I recommend are listed below and in the Bibliography. But, ultimately, experience is the best teacher. That is why it is so important to look for ways to gain experience at a low risk. It is far better to learn OOAD on a short-term pilot project than on a long-term, expensive one. Believe me, I know.

References

Booch, Grady. *Object-Oriented Analysis and Design with Applications* (2nd edition). Redwood City, Calif.: Benjamin/Cummings Publishing Co., 1994.

Carmichael, Andy (ed.). *Object Development Methods*. New York: SIGS Books, 1994.

Coad, Peter, and Edward Yourdon, *Object-Oriented* Analysis (2nd edition). Englewood Cliffs, N.J.: Yourdon Press, 1991.

Coleman, Derek, with Patrick Arnold, Stephanie Bodoff, Chris Dollin, Helena Gilchrist, Fiona Hayes and Paul Jeremaes. *Object-Oriented Development: The Fusion Method*. Englewood Cliffs, N.J.: Prentice-Hall, 1994.

DeMarco, Tom, and Timothy Lister, *Peopleware*. New York: Dorset House Publishing, 1987.

Firesmith, Donald G. *Object-Oriented Requirements Analysis and Logical Design: A Software Engineering Approach*. New York: John Wiley & Sons, 1993.

Jacobson, Ivar, with Magnus Christerson, Patrik Jonsson, and Gunnar Övergaard. *Object-Oriented Software Engineering: A Use Case Driven Approach (4th printing)*. Reading, Mass.: ACM Press/Addison-Wesley, 1992.

Rumbaugh, James, with Michael Blaha, William Premerlani, Frederick Eddy, and William Lorensen. *Object-Oriented Modeling and Design*. Englewood Cliffs, N.J.: Prentice-Hall, 1991.

Shlaer, Sally, and Stephen J. Mellor. *Object Lifecycles: Modeling the World in States*. Englewood Cliffs, N.J.: Yourdon Press, 1992.

Sullo, Gary C. *Object Engineering: Designing Large-Scale Object-Oriented Systems*. New York: John Wiley & Sons, 1994.

Wilkie, George. *Object-Oriented Software Engineering*. Reading, Mass.: Addison-Wesley, 1993.

Wirfs-Brock, Rebecca, with Brian Wilkerson and Lauren Wiener. *Designing Object-Oriented Software*. Englewood Cliffs, N.J.: PTR Prentice-Hall, 1990.

CHAPTER 5:

ENVIRONMENT, LANGUAGE, AND TOOL PITFALLS

"We dissect nature along lines laid down by our native language...Language is not simply a reporting device for experience but a defining framework for it."

— Benjamin Whorf, "Thinking in Primitive Communities," Hoyer (ed.), *New Directions in the Study of Language*, 1964.

Environments, languages, and tools make up probably the most controversial area of object-oriented development, as well as the one most subject to change as time goes on.

Early drafts of this chapter had a lengthy discussion of environments and frameworks such as Microsoft's OLE 2.0, the Novell-Apple-IBM OpenDoc initiative, NeXT's NEXTSTEP, the OpenStep standard proposed by NeXT and SunSoft, Taligent's CommonPoint, Microsoft's proposed Cairo environment, and so on. However, during the time between drafts it became apparent how much things would and could change. So I cut back on evaluations and observations, choosing instead to use specific cases only as examples.

Environments comprise the operating systems and application environments in which a given project will run: Windows, IBM's OS/2, Apple's Mac OS, the various flavors of UNIX, NEXTSTEP, OpenStep, Taligent, and so on.

Languages include the various object-oriented (and not-so-object oriented) languages used to implement your object design: Smalltalk, C++, Eiffel, Objective-C, CLOS, Object Pascal, and so on.

Tools are what you use to create and test the implementation: editors, compilers, browsers, interface builders, object database management systems (ODBMS), source code management (SCM) systems, computer-aided software engineering (CASE) packages, and so on.

The boundaries between the three aren't always clear; for example, Smalltalk and Eiffel implementations are often a combination of application environment and tools, centered on a language. Likewise, one can argue which category an object request broker (ORB) falls into. But regardless of category, these items are what allow you to carry out object-oriented development, so you need to choose them wisely and use them well.

Pitfall 5.1: Targeting the wrong environment for commercial applications.

If you're creating an object-oriented commercial application—one for sale to other firms rather than for in-house deployment—you must first define your market. That may sound obvious, but many firms start out with a nifty idea, develop it for the environment they think best, and then quietly fold, unable to win sufficient number of customers.

Although it's possible to do object-oriented development for a non-OO operating system, such as Windows or Macintosh, you face significant challenges. You may realize few benefits of OOD because the system doesn't mesh well with it. The system itself may demand application architectures that don't readily fit into an object-oriented mold. And the major non-OO operating systems already have mature, entrenched application products in nearly every significant category.

Object-oriented environments (OOE), such as NEXTSTEP, OpenStep, and Taligent, generally facilitate object-oriented development. If you design and implement well, you should get significant leverage from the environment itself. However, the OOE may not have the customer base to support your firm, in which case you're in big trouble.

Symptoms   For non-OOE: few of the expected benefits from object-oriented development; significant challenges in development; high cost of marketing (for Windows). For OOE: a too small installed base of potential customers; slow growth of installed base; withdrawal of other major applications from the environment.

Consequences   Product failure and possibly even company failure. This is a serious pitfall, and one that has trapped and will continue to trap many software companies.

Detection   For a non-OOE, track how well development is holding to schedule. In the meantime, do as much market research as you can afford. Keep a close eye on entrenched products and large competitors.

For an OOE, push long and hard on the originating company for reference accounts, potential customers, and trustworthy numbers for installed base. Stay focused on how the environment is being deployed and used.

Extraction   Hard reset: Select a new environment (either for deployment or to target for development) and move ahead as quickly as possible.

Prevention   This is one key to company success. The truth is that it's a tough market for commercial software vendors, and the market continues to transform, in some cases between the time a project begins and when it ships. What's more, a "common sense" answer might lead you to abandon the attempt altogether, while others who push ahead might find that the right break appears along the way.

Pitfall 5.2: Deploying the wrong environment in-house.

This pitfall specifically refers to selecting the operating system or application environment to be deployed in-house in conjunction with reengineering of legacy mainframe applications, as well as development and deployment of mission-critical custom applications (MCCAs) created using object-oriented development.

This decision may well be out of your hands—for example, company management may dictate what desktop environment is to be deployed—but if it isn't, then you have careful thinking to do.

You can face several hard choices. Do you select and deploy a specific object-oriented environment, or do you stay with the operating system already deployed? If you choose to use an OOE, which one do you pick? Do you maintain access to legacy productivity applications and data, or do you try to convert them somehow? If you don't choose an OOE, then how fast can your object-oriented development proceed, and will you get all the benefits you need?

This pitfall is fraught with dangers in four areas: technology, compatibility, economics, and politics. Technology refers to the benefits, real or touted, of a given environment. Compatibility refers to how well currently used ("legacy") environments, applications, data, and skills can be integrated with the new environment and applications. Economics refers to all the costs associated with a given choice, including those for licensing fees, necessary hardware upgrades or replacements, compatible applications, end-user training, and possible lost productivity during conversion. Politics refers to the various reasons—apart from technology, compatibility, or economics—that people might support or resist a given selection, ranging from instinct to prejudice to ulterior motives. A decision might make perfect sense for any three of the areas, but be doomed because of problems in the fourth.

Symptoms   For an OOE: constantly slipping ship date; constant problems with lack of available tools or applications; significant bugs; withdrawal or lack of updates for key productivity applications.

For a non-OOE: no perceived benefits from OOD; significant problems in development and deployment.

Consequences   Major losses in time, money, and productivity for the group, division, or company that is doing the deployment. And you might lose your job.

Detection   Make a list of any current or incipient problems in each of the four areas above (technology, compatibility, economics, and politics). Then make a list of the current demonstrable benefits in each of the four areas. The longer the first list and the shorter the second, the more likely that you've picked the wrong environment.

Extraction   There are two solutions: Stay with the original choice or make a new one. If you stay with the original choice, then you must focus on whittling down the list of problems while actively expanding the list of demonstrable benefits. In some cases, this can be the easier choice, because many other people may also have an investment in continuing with it; but it is not necessarily the best one for the company in those four areas.

If you decide to go with a new environment, be prepared for some real difficulties. Those who favor the current choice will oppose the switch, and those who did not want the current choice will berate you for having picked it in the first place.

Prevention   You have hard choices to make. For each environment (or combination of environments) being considered, evaluate it in the four given areas, listing pros and cons and noting the relative importance of each (assign a value from 0 to 10). This process will help you to identify potential problems in advance.

Next, if it is feasible (and it may not be, for reasons of company confidentiality), find other companies that have deployed the environments you're considering. Be sure to ask the opinions of at least three key groups: the business managers (who worry about business benefits), the MIS managers (who support the environment and deal with legacy issues), and the users (who work with the environment all day long).

Having done all this, rank each of the environments based on potential risks and potential benefits. At this point, the choice may be clear, or it may be a toss-up between two or more environments. In either case, you must now start to work to build consensus among the same groups in your own firm (business managers, personnel, MIS, users). If you have the luxury of both time and money to spend, do a trial deployment. But keep your resume up-to-date.

Pitfall 5.3: Believing manufacturers' claims about object orientation.

Manufacturers of various environments, languages, and tools would have you believe that their products are object-oriented, implying that you will gain the benefits of object-oriented development by using their products. Unfortunately, that's not always the case.

For example, Microsoft used to tout version 2.0 of its object linking and embedding (OLE) system as being object-oriented. If you believe that, then you might approach OLE 2.0 expecting rapid development, better management of complexity, and significant code reuse. You might even expect OOD features such as inheritance and subclassing.

Unfortunately, Microsoft's claims that OLE 2.0 is object-oriented were reminiscent of ripping the roof off a car and calling it a convertible. There are some vague similarities—for example, the way a given "Microsoft object" (Microsoft's term, not mine) can support several standard predefined interfaces is a bit like using mixin classes in C++ or (more closely) protocols in Objective-C. But OLE does not use hierarchy and inheritance; without that, the best you have are abstract data types. Instead of giving you the benefits of OOD, OLE 2.0 is a programming nightmare, as you can learn from many independent software vendors (ISVs) developing for it.

In a similar fashion, other vendors may claim object orientation for their products, often for reasons as simple (and fatuous) as an iconic drag-and-drop interface.

Symptoms   Taking on faith anything a vendor says about its products being object-oriented. Assuming that development using its products will yield classic OOD benefits.

Consequences   A rude awakening as development proceeds. Potentially major schedule slippage.

Detection   Note the assumptions that developers, technical managers, and upper management are making about the various environments, languages, and tools being used. If they are cautious or (better yet) dubious, you're probably safe. If they're enthusiastic, you may have problems.

Extraction   Reset everyone's expectations, including your own. Decide whether you have to use these products; replan and reschedule accordingly.

Prevention   There are certainly disagreements about what makes something object-oriented, and even over whether inheritance is essential to the category. We need also to distinguish between whether a given product is object-oriented in and of itself, and whether it allows you to do object-oriented development. For example, a given compiler for an object-oriented language may not be object-oriented in and of itself, and that might not matter at all.

If a product isn't object-oriented when you need or want it to be, can you always ignore or avoid it? Sometimes not. For example, if you're developing a commercial Windows productivity application or utility, then you're going to have to support OLE 2.0. Like it or not, OLE 2.0 and the Win32 API are Microsoft's announced standards for current and future Windows-based environments. Just be aware of what benefits a given product or environment will really give you.

Pitfall 5.4: Using C++.

It's not hard to find critics of C++ within the object development community. Programmer and author Henry Spencer called C++ "the best example of second system effect since OS/360." Douglas Kahn and Jeff Sutherland noted that C++ definitely isn't the "silver bullet" that developers and managers have sought. McCabe and Watson observed that "cleverness is not a prerequisite for incomprehensibility in C++." Lorenz and Kidd noted that their metric for average person-days per class shows much higher values for C++ than for Smalltalk, in part because "C++ is more cryptic and difficult to reuse, resulting in more reinvention versus reuse." Lily notes that "the inability to use [C++] as it was intended is a serious hurdle" in achieving the potential of object-oriented development. Goldberg cited IS managers who said one of the worst things to do in making the transition to object technology was "to learn about objects by learning to program, and to do so in C++." (Check the References at the end of this chapter for the particulars on these pronouncements.)

C++ is hard to learn. If you don't believe me, take the word of Philippe Kahn—president, chairman, and CEO of Borland International, a major vendor of C++ compilers. At the keynote panel of the 1994 ObjectWorld conference, Kahn stated outright that C++ is hard to learn, that few programmers get really good at it, and that his company was looking for ways to develop products to help programmers be more productive in C++.

C++ has subtle and often hard-to-predict behaviors. Consider the issue of initialization, copying, and assignment of objects. C++ will generate for a given class a default constructor, a copy constructor, and an assignment operator if you fail to do so yourself. A new C++ programmer—especially one familiar with ANSI C—will need time to learn when each of these member functions is called, particularly with reference to declaring, defining, initializing and assigning variables. Different sequences of such statements that were equivalent in ANSI C can have quite different results in C++.

C++ lacks true dynamic binding—deferral of object class resolution until run time. At first, C++ proponents argued that dynamic binding was dangerous and inefficient, citing the benefits of compile-time type-checking. Then they added virtual methods, which provide a kind of run time binding—but only when you're dealing with a pointer to a known class with a declared virtual method. The most recent effort to rectify things is the proposal for run-time type information (RTTI), which has all the problems inherent to retrofitting a capability for which the language was not intended. In the meantime, other object-oriented languages designed in dynamic binding from the start and handle it in a clean, rational, predictable way.

In short, C++ is a significant barrier to learning and correctly applying object-oriented methodologies and techniques.

Symptoms Developers spending lots of time tracking down obscure and pernicious bugs related more to C++ than to OOD or the problem at hand; developers spending time looking for ways to code around C++ restrictions or limitations.

Consequences Lots of time spent teaching developers to use C++ properly. A high rate of bugs. Schedule slips and missed milestones. Programmers resigning in disgust.

Detection Survey your developers to see how much time they feel they're spending dealing with C++ instead of project design and implementation. At the same time, conduct selected code reviews, involving someone who is very good at C++, to identify any common flaws or errors in approach.

Extraction If you're in the middle of a project using C++, chances are that you won't have the opportunity to switch languages. In that case, your only option is to improve everyone's C++ skills. The top two books I recommend are *Effective C++* by Scott Meyers, and *The Taligent Guide to Writing Effective Programs*, by Taligent, Inc., both published by Addison-Wesley. Meyers' book offers 50 rules on how to properly use C++, with a strong focus on OOD. The Taligent book takes much the same tack; even ignoring the chapters specific to Taligent development, you're still left with a useful core of accumulated wisdom and insight on OOD using C++.

Prevention You may not be able to avoid using C++ (see next pitfall). If you can't, be prepared to recruit all the available expert C++ developers you can find, and there aren't many; remember Webster's Constant: The number of excellent developers in a new area of technology quickly reaches a constant value, which is sustained through the period during which the technology is vital. As for the other engineers, be prepared to spend time before and during development training them in proper C++ development. Be sure to adopt a rigorous canonical class form and set of development rules.

Pitfall 5.5: Not using C++.

As cathartic as the previous pitfall might be for some of us, the truth is that C++ is the closest thing to a standard among the object-oriented programming languages (OOPLs) in the world today. It is the most broadly supported, has the greatest variety of compilers and supporting tools, and is considered the standard development language for SunSoft's DOE, OS/2, the OpenDoc initiative, Taligent, and Windows.

Tom Love put it well in his book *Object Lessons*: "The competition in the marketplace is now well aligned with object-oriented languages. Apple is using two languages: C++ and Dylan. Sun and Hewlett-Packard are using C++. NeXT is using Objective-C. IBM is using C++ and Smalltalk. How would you bet?"

That pretty much sums up the bottom line. As much as you might like Smalltalk or Object Pascal or Eiffel or Objective-C or Object Cobol or even Dylan, C++ is still the most common, most supported, and most portable OOPL. This doesn't mean that you have to use C++—there are still compelling reasons to use other OOPLs—but you need to make your decision with due consideration.

There are three significant risks in not using C++. The first is that your project may not integrate as well into the host environment or with other tools or applications. Second, the language you use may not be well-supported or even available if you try to port your project to another environment; in some cases, the support of the language in your current environment may be at risk. The third risk is that you may end up having to convert your project to C++ in the end.

Symptoms   Poor integration into target environment; constant workarounds required; few sources for development environments and tools.

Consequences   Lack of portability; poor coordination with other applications; problems with availability and quality of tools; poor performance.

Detection   This pitfall is hard to detect, because it means evaluating the situation based on outside market and technological trends. In many cases, you are better off staying with your current OOPL until the project is finished (see below). The ultimate consideration: List all the possible consequences, with relative probability, if you continue with your OOPL; then list the consequences if you switch to C++.

Extraction   Many of the OOPLs support integration with C++ code, so your first step could be to rewrite key classes and subsystems in C++, one at a time. If that's feasible, then continue that process, converting larger and larger chunks to C++.

If that integration doesn't exist, then you need to make some hard decisions about whether to restart in C++ or push ahead to completion, with the goal of starting a C++ conversion afterward. Software engineering argues for the latter course; you'll end up with both a better project and a better C++ implementation if you complete the project once, and then rewrite it in C++, as opposed to switching to C++ in midstream.

Prevention   Evaluate carefully your reasons for using another OOPL instead of C++. These reasons may be compelling, and you may stand a better chance of success; see Pitfall 5.4. But recognize that you may be setting barriers for yourself that may come back to haunt you later. All things being equal, you may be better off in the long run—commercially, not technically—going with C++.

Pitfall 5.6: Not investing in supporting tools and training.

Yes, it's possible to do object-oriented development with nothing more than an editor, a compiler, and a debugger. It's also possible to build a house with a hammer, a saw, and a plane. The question in both cases is: why would you want to? Given the tools that are available for object-oriented development, why shackle yourself by not using them? Yet companies often drag their feet or refuse to evaluate and adopt OOD tools.

The two main excuses given are cost and utility. The various tools available to support OOD tend to be pricey, typically in the range of $500 to $5,000 per developer-seat license. (It's telling when you can look through an issue of, say, *Object Magazine* and be hard-pressed to find a single ad that gives a product price.) Market pressures are driving some prices down, but there is a lower limit, because there is no mass market for OOD tools.

Recognize that you'll need to invest time and money in training to go along with the tools. It doesn't make sense to purchase these tools and have them used poorly or haphazardly, if at all.

Beyond the equipment price are other costs, including conversion of existing work methods to adopt the tools, and risks associated with the tool's quality, completeness, and continued life.

The utility issue reflects concerns about whether the tool will do the job you need in the environment in which it is used. Will it show a measurable improvement in the area it is meant to improve (design quality, code quality, productivity, and so on)?

The cost and utility issues are genuine but are often used as a smokescreen. Utility can be judged by trial use and talks with reference accounts. As for cost, the amount spent on tools is small compared with what the company loses for each week or month that a project is late or, for that matter, compared with what the company spends each year on each developer.

Symptoms   Constant denial of funds for evaluating and purchasing OOD tools.

Consequences   Lower productivity; design and implementation weaknesses; longer development times.

Detection   Evaluate the current tools used. Ask the developers what would be an ideal set of tools to help them be more productive. Make a trial proposal to evaluate and adopt tools. See if whether gets shot down or sidetracked.

Extraction   Do research to see what tools might be of use; you may be able to get inexpensive evaluation copies and names of existing users. Make a demonstrable case for benefits, focusing on meeting project schedule. Go for one tool at a time, possibly with limited deployment.

Prevention   When possible, do the research in **Detection** and **Extraction** before the project starts. Make a list of the specific tools needed for each developer; not all developers will need all tools. In many cases, floating network licenses can be purchased for a given number of users, so tools that aren't often used won't need a large number of licenses.

Many tools can be developed in-house. This is generally a more expensive proposition for tools of any complexity, but the resulting tools are specific to your needs. Any development organization worth its salt should have at least one developer devoted part- or full-time to tool creation and support.

Conclusion

If you're going for commercial volume or if you want to write the next great killer application, then logic says to use C++ to develop an OLE-compliant Windows application. The question is, will you be able to finish it, and will anyone buy it if you do?

On the other hand, if you're writing an in-house, custom application, you may have the luxury of picking the environment and language best suited to your needs and demands. The question in this case is, will you later regret having done so?

It boils down to this: Selection of the target environment and language for object-oriented development is perhaps the single greatest pitfall—and there may be no way out of or around this one. Your best shot is to choose carefully from an informed vantage point, seeking real-world experience and feedback from others.

References

Goldberg, Adele. "Wishful thinking, *Object Magazine* 3(2), Jul/Aug 1993.

Kahn, R. Douglas and Jeff, Sutherland. "Let's start under-promising and over-delivering on object technology," *Object Magazine* 4(1), Mar/Apr 1994.

Lily, Susan. "Is object-oriented programming harmful?" *Object Magazine* 3(2), Jul/Aug 1993.

Lorenz, Mark and Jeff Kidd. *Object-Oriented Software Metrics*. Englewood Cliffs, N.J.: Prentice-Hall, 1994.

Love, Tom. *Object Lessons*. New York: SIGS Books, 1993.

McCabe, Thomas J. and Arthur H. Watson. "Combining comprehension and testing in object-oriented development," *Object Magazine* 4(1), Mar/Apr 1994.

Meyers, Scott. *Effective* C++. Reading, Mass.: Addison-Wesley, 1992.

Taligent, Inc. *Taligent's Guide to Designing Programs*. Reading, Mass.: Addison-Wesley, 1994.

Webster, Bruce. *The Art of 'Ware* New York: M&T Books, in press.

CHAPTER 6:

IMPLEMENTATION PITFALLS

Had I been present at the Creation,
I would have given some useful hints for the better ordering of the universe.

— Alfonso the Wise, King of Castile (1221-1284)

Somewhere between design, tools, and writing the objects themselves are development practices that can lead engineers into pitfalls.

If there's a theme common to the pitfalls in this chapter, it's that object-oriented development often tempts us to do what we want, rather than what we ought. Whether it's jumping feet-first into coding, flitting off to the next feature, or getting caught up in seeing what clever hacks we can concoct from the language and environment, we let ourselves be seduced by the easy and entertaining path.

The heart of the problem is this: *The task that we least want to tackle is probably the one we need to focus most on.* Self-discipline is essential to solid software engineering, and that applies all the more for object-oriented development. It takes education, discipline, and practice to do excellent object-oriented development, but the payoff will be greater.

Pitfall 6.1: Coding too soon.

Like many of the others, this pitfall is not unique to object-oriented development. In fact, it is pandemic to software engineering and has been addressed repeatedly over the past thirty years.

As noted in Pitfall 4.1, engineers are drawn to the power of creation that software development grants them. The media they use are malleable and ephemeral to a degree previously unknown in human history. Fifty years of tool development, language refinement, system evolution, and hardware advances has given software developers the power to build little worlds and universes (figuratively and literally), tear them down, and then build new ones with little waste or loss. The emotional and intellectual rush associated with creating working software is powerful and addictive; it's little wonder that so many faults and failings come from neglecting other software engineering activities.

Object-oriented development intensifies the high. The concepts, tools, languages, and environments give engineers even greater power of creation because of common OOD factors such as rapid prototyping, code and design reuse, and greater management of complexity. Put another way, once engineers understand object concepts, they find it far easier to envision architecture and implementation, with code straining to pour out of their fingertips.

The real danger is that coding too soon can appear to work for a while (see Pitfall 6.3), and often there is little immediate feedback telling engineers that they're on the wrong path. And because the resulting progress (apparent or real) pleases others, especially upper management, it can be hard to counter or correct this tendency.

Symptoms   Engineers coding before sufficient analysis and design are completed.

Consequences   Neglect of analysis and design. Establishment of inappropriate architecture and feature implementation. Schedule slip due to redesign and reimplementation later in the project.

Detection   Refer to recommendations in Pitfall 4.1 to check whether analysis and design have been sufficiently completed. Then survey the engineers to see how many are actually coding already.

Extraction   Halt coding until analysis and design are sufficiently complete. Shift to an iterative development cycle, in which each cycle contains analysis, design, implementation, and testing; this spreads coding over several cycles and allows a greater check on what's being written.

Prevention

Too often we fail to develop a high sense of creation, merit, and professionalism about analysis and design. Compounding that is upper management's desire to see active results, combined with their frequent suspicion that engineers are goofing off. Upper management must not only tolerate and support delays of coding until analysis and design are finished, but they must demand it; likewise, engineering teams need to develop a professional attitude about ensuring that proper analysis and design are complete before a line of code is typed.

Having said all that, I do recognize the value of prototyping, which often involves coding. But prototyping too often leads to its own pitfalls (see Pitfalls 1.9, 3.9, 6.3, 6.5) and so should be used with strict guidelines in place.

Pitfall 6.2: Assuming that encapsulation obviates design and implementation standards.

As noted in Pitfall 4.6, object development teams often conclude that class and subsystem encapsulation, which hides the implementation behind a public interface, eliminates any issues about the implementation itself. The idea is that as long as the interface remains constant or changes only through proper review procedures, it doesn't matter how the class or subsystem is implemented.

It does matter, however.

First, few (if any) object-oriented programming languages can completely express programmatically the interface for a given class or subsystem. The interface is more than a list of all the methods and their parameters. It also includes all the explicit and implied invariants, such as assumed preconditions and resulting postconditions for each method. It includes the ranges and combinations of acceptable values for incoming parameters. It includes all the possible valid states for a given object or subsystem and the circumstances under which the interface should assume each state. And it includes all system consequences; constraints on timing and circumstances under which a given method can be called; and behavior associated with each state.

Second, any subclass of a given class must either preserve these invariants or document how it overrides them. Encapsulation notwithstanding, the subclass needs to know enough about implementation in order to correctly override or extend behavior in a correct and predictable manner. Without the ability to do this, code reuse—the single most touted benefit of object-oriented development—cannot be achieved to any great extent.

Third, no matter how loose the coupling between any two objects or subsystems, the chances of bugs in that coupling are inversely proportional to the degree of architectural and coding unity between them.

Finally, no code is an island. Because of the factors discussed above, because we are writing complex systems based on components, because we need to get into each other's code to make connections and fix bugs, because we no longer stay with the same company for long periods of time, and because we don't want to keep working with the same code forever, we need to ensure that others can, as readily as possible, pick up where we left off.

Symptoms   Boundary errors between objects and subsystems. Engineers complaining about another's code. High bug counts, with a steady stream of new ones.

Consequences   Poor integration between classes and between subsystems. Project instability. Late projects, buggy features. Little code reuse.

Detection   First, simply ask yourself, Do we have a chief architect? Do we have design and implementation standards? Do we have coding standards? If the answers are negative, then you'll almost certainly have this problem. If the answers are all yes but you suspect that the problem exists anyway, hold a code review, with the chief architect asking the questions about standards and implementation.

Extraction   This is another "pay now, or pay later with interest and penalty" situation. If you're far along in a project, you may want to push to completion and then appoint a chief architect and define standards for implementing and enforcing the *next* project. However, you run the risk of suffering significant delays in the current project.

Prevention   The answer is simple, though not necessarily easy: Define standards and enforce them. The steps to do this include the following:

- Conduct sufficient analysis and design.
- Appoint and empower a chief architect (perhaps a small team for a large project).
- Define design, implementation, documentation, and coding standards for subsystems and classes.
- Use regular design and code reviews to ensure compliance.

Pitfall 6.3: Being fooled by the illusion of rapid progress.

This pitfall has shown up in different forms for both upper management (Pitfall 1.9) and technical management (Pitfall 3.9), but it can happen to developers, too. Tremendous exhilaration can occur during the rapid development when you use a good object-oriented development environment with good class libraries (especially for user interfaces) and other supporting tools. You can set up class hierarchies and fill out class definitions in a matter of days or even hours. You can rapidly add and modify features. You can imagine everything getting done faster than you had dared hope.

You can be really, really wrong.

Because it was so fast and easy to create an object class or get a basic feature working, you can be fooled into thinking that completing the task will be just as fast and easy. This is especially true if you don't have a complete specification or if you don't know what the complete specification is. What you often find, however, is that it's like setting up a nice component stereo system in a great cabinet and then finding that you still need to build the circuitry and other electronics within each component. The pretty job went fast, was easy, and looked good; the effort and tedium of implementing all the nitty-gritty details is less attractive and can easily be avoided or ignored.

Symptoms   Consistently underestimating the time required for completion of a given feature, aspect, or subsystem.

Consequences   Schedule slippage; lack of ability to make reliable schedules and estimates; loss of credibility.

Detection   For a given class, subsystem, or feature, write down how much time you expect it will take to complete. For each item, identify and write down every detail about what remains to be done. Then record how much time you estimate each detail will require. Add it all up. Compare the sum to your original assumption. If there's a significant difference, you have problems.

Extraction   Use the detail list with estimates as a starting point. Do a design and code review for the particular item. Revise your detail list and estimates if necessary. If you are responsible for multiple items, repeat the process for each item, noting any interdependencies. Also note whether you depend on someone else's efforts. Try to lay out an actual day-by-day schedule to complete all the details of all the classes, subsystems, and features. Add 20 percent. Now add 20 percent more. Use that as an estimate for how long it will take you to get all your work done. Project management software may help to automate the process; resist the temptation, though, to collapse many items into a few.

Prevention   Follow the process described in **Detection** and **Extraction**. Take the time up front to design, describe, and estimate each task in significant detail. Have someone else go through what you've done and point out anything you've forgotten and overlooked.

This is, frankly, a wretched process to go through, but it will pay off in the end...provided, of course, that your managers (or their managers) are willing to accept the brutally honest schedule you give.

Pitfall 6.4: Making too many promises without having enough time to keep them.

As developers, we tend to want to please those who have hopes or expectations of us. We do this for several reasons. We like to think of ourselves as exceptionally capable. We don't like saying that we won't be able to do something. We may think that what's being asked is so trivial that it won't affect things much. We may be worried about our next job review or even keeping our current job.

Because of these factors, there is a real temptation to just say, "Sure!" when someone asks us to do something. This is especially true in object-oriented development, because we can often immediately think of how we would implement what's being asked. And the request may truly be minor.

The problem is twofold. Every request, no matter how minor, adds to the development schedule. It may literally take only a matter of minutes to make the initial code changes, but even such trivial modifications often have ramifications that can ripple for a long time, becasue of testing requirements and interactions with other code.

The second problem is that these change requests add up. A day here, a day there, and pretty soon you're adding weeks to your delivery schedule.

Symptoms A growing list of commitments and a sense of panic over when you'll get time to complete them all.

Consequences Constant schedule slippage. Trade-offs between formal commitments and informal ones. Frustration and anger from those to whom you made promises.

Detection Make a list of all such promises. Note how many there are. Add to the list as you remember additional ones. Write down your conservative estimate of how long it will take to fully implement each one. See how the rest of your schedule accommodates that.

Extraction Go back to those to whom you've made promises and tell them, "I'm sorry, but I'm facing major schedule problems, so we'll have to handle your request through formal channels. Please discuss any changes you require with my manager."

Prevention   Just say no. Have a formal process for handling requests for changes, no matter how small, and make those who want changes to go through that process. If the team has a technical manager, she should handle all change requests. She should also know that you're focused on your official tasks and that any special requests will always come at the expense of the current schedule.

Pitfall 6.5: Leaving the details for later.

Given a standard format for your object classes, it's easy to quickly lay out both the interface (with all the declarations) and the implementation (with the actual definitions). Basic functionality can also be written quickly. Inheritance often makes the new class quite capable. Usually, there are three or four methods that you implement as dummy or simple methods with some basic functionality. You test it some and then move on to the next class.

This process sounds quick and easy, and sometimes it's an effective way to set up development. But failing to complete the class implementation can lead to several problems. You may forget some of your original design intentions and then may have trouble remembering what to do when you come back to complete the class. You might introduce bugs and other instabilities into the system. Or you might simply forget to come back and finish things.

The most serious problem, though, is that we tend to avoid—put off—the task that is most tedious and difficult, which is often why we don't finish the details right away. This means, of course, that the aspects of each class or subsystem that we are most likely to delay completing are those that will be the hardest to complete and that will have the highest risk. Assuming that this is happening for every class and subsystem that you're coding, you are building a growing mass of the most difficult tasks, which will have to be handled toward the end of the development cycle—when they do the most damage to the project schedule and architecture.

Symptoms   Looking at a given class or subsystem and telling yourself, "I'll finish that later." Getting evasive answers from other engineers when you ask them about given features or deliverables. Chronic lack of progress in a given feature or subsystem.

Consequences   Major schedule and design impact late in the development cycle, resulting in schedule slip or loss of planned features.

Detection   Examine each class or subsystem. Make a detailed list of all that remains to be done. Ask yourself why you haven't done those tasks yet. Then ask yourself when—specifically—you will actually start doing the items on the list. If you're a manager, have each engineer do this.

Extraction   Make a list of all your unfinished classes and subsystems and rate each of them according to difficulty and significance. Pick the hardest, nastiest one and make it your top priority. Work on it until it's either finished or you're absolutely, honestly blocked. Then work on the next one on the list. And so on.

Prevention   Use the process described in **Extraction**. When you start to implement a given class or subsystem, work on it until it is either complete or absolutely blocked. Note that "complete" may mean finished in terms of the development goals for this cycle, as opposed to the final target functionality; but don't use that as an excuse to skimp. If anything, seek to overachieve.

Pitfall 6.6: Rewriting subsystems in a single bound.

One of the advantages of object-oriented development is your ability to rapidly rewrite classes and subsystems. You can do this several ways:

- By keeping the interfaces the same and changing all the details of the implementation.
- By rearranging the connections between various object instances.
- By making changes to the class interfaces and appropriately updating any calling classes.
- By reorganizing the class hierarchy, pushing identified general behavior further up, making new subclasses, or even by changing class lineage.

With skill and care, you can do all this quickly and get the new code to recompile and link in readily.

Unfortunately, this capability can also be one of the disadvantages of OOD. It can be the design equivalent of "code-and-go" programming, where you run into a bug, jump into the source code, change a few lines, recompile, and see if that fixed the problem—and then repeat the process if that didn't fix things. The correct approach to debugging code is to track down the source of the problem, figure out why the bug appeared in the first place, and make the correct and complete changes to solve that problem. But this method is often ignored when you're dealing with class and subsystem issues in OOD.

Symptoms   High code turnover in specific classes and subsystems. Sudden changes to class interface and hierarchy.

Consequences   Instability of classes and subsystems. Long delay times getting a particular subsystem to work. Weak implementations.

Detection   The first method of detection is to monitor yourself (if you're writing code). When you find yourself wanting to redesign a class or subsystem, ask yourself some searching questions about why you want to do it and what the alternatives are.

For projectwide monitoring, set up a system (preferably automated) to track indications of source code changes for each class or subsystem in the project. This system should track on a daily or weekly basis the change in total number of lines of code for each source code file—the amount by which the file shrank or grew—as well as the number of lines of code that were modified. With those two metrics, you can see where the effort is going, and it can flag the files being worked on the most.

Extraction   If you find that you or others have been rewriting too often, you need to call the situation to everyone's attention. Then get a group commitment to follow the steps outlined below in **Prevention**.

Prevention   Establish ahead of time a formal or informal process to follow when you think that a class or subsystem rewrite may be necessary:

1. First, stop. Resist the temptation to rewrite until this process is complete.

2. Think hard and identify the real problem and the real solution. See how many alternative solutions you can devise. Choose the best.

3. Write down your proposed actions.

4. Review your written report with other engineers and particularly with the chief architect; listen to what they have to say.

5. Plan your rewriting strategy. If you can, implement it as a series of steps so that you can test the results at each step and have a clear path to back out should that be necessary.

By codifying this process—in essence, making it part of your development methodology—you help to reduce unnecessary or misdirected rewrites.

Pitfall 6.7: Failing to document and remember key concepts and decisions.

Object-oriented development often involves lots of discussion, interaction, and brainstorming about architecture, class hierarchy, class design, connections between classes, and so on. This process becomes common—and critical—when you're discussing which classes to create, what the hierarchy should look like, how classes and subsystems are supposed to work, and so on. As noted elsewhere, many of the semantics of class and subsystem interfaces are not contained in the actual source code, but are instead embodied in the intent of the developer.

An engineer may have a set of reasons, carefully thought out, as to why a class or subsystem was designed and implemented in a certain way and may have formulated long-term intentions for that component. However, as time goes on, the engineer may forget some of the decisions and plans behind that design and implementation. Engineers are not known for their eagerness to carefully and meticulously write down plans and procedures, so there's a good chance that the concepts behind design choices will be lost—possibly for good, but at least until the engineer needs to remember them and can re-create them as closely as possible.

In the meantime, other engineers may likewise forget or even be ignorant of those concepts and reasons. They form their own assumptions as best they can, based on the code interface and whatever factors the original engineer remembers and communicates. The result is a type of genetic drift in design and implementation.

Symptoms   Periodically "reinventing the wheel." Systems that don't fit together as well as they should. Planned features dropping out.

Consequences   Wasted time spent repairing design and implementation; schedule slippage; loss of functionality.

Detection   Gather together all the engineers. Go through the class hierarchy. For each class, ask, "Why did we choose to create this class and implement it this way?" Ask about data and function members in that class. See what decisions you begin to flush out. If you keep coming up with statements like, "Well, our original intent was to..."

or "I thought we were going to make it do this...", then you probably have significant lost decisions.

Extraction   Do a design review of the project, class by class. For each class, document all the assumptions, decisions, trade-offs, and reasoning that went into designing that class. If necessary, do the same on both higher (subsystem) and lower (method) levels.

Prevention   Require that an on-line document be created for every class, justifying its creation and its design and explaining the assumptions behind it as well as future plans for use and expansion. Require that engineers who are significantly modifying a given class also appropriately revise the corresponding document. Review the documents regularly to remind yourself of what decisions and plans you may have forgotten.

Pitfall 6.8: Being seduced by the dark side.

Use of an object-oriented programming language(OOPL) by no means guarantees that the classes and systems you create will be well formed and will follow solid practices of either object-oriented development or software engineering in general. Put another way, you have plenty of rope with which to hang yourself. Indeed, you may also have several new scaffolds and a greater variety of knots.

When engineers start using their first OOPL, they quickly discover that they have a whole new set of tools to work with, such as inheritance, polymorphism, virtual methods, upcasting, downcasting, dynamic binding, and so on. Many engineers then knowingly use those tools in ways they were never intended to be used, and that violate any number of OOD tenets. They excuse their efforts in the name of expediency, necessity, or even just because the challenge or opportunity is there.

There are situations that require you to break the rules, but it should only be done with approval and after careful consideration. Otherwise, you will lose portability, reliability, and the ability to reuse code.

Symptoms Persistent, hard-to-detect bugs. Engineers who keep saying things like, "Wanna see the neat hack I did with multiple inheritance?"

Consequences Code instability. Lack of portability. Long test and debug cycles. Shipment slippage.

Detection To detect problems, you first have to decide what the problems are (see **Prevention,** below). Having done that, share the list with engineers and ask for their comments. Note who says, "Why can't I do that?" Note who says, "That's funny—So-and-so does that all the time." And so on.

Extraction Decide what practices are acceptable and which aren't (see **Prevention,** below). Do a code review to identify violations. Implement a regular cross-check on source code; have engineers look at each other's code weekly. Clean up each violation found, if possible.

Prevention Establish programming idiom standards, particularly with regard to object-oriented development. Two good starting places for ideas are *Taligent's Guide to Designing Programs* and *Effective C++* (see

References at the end of this chapter). Have a clear list of practices to follow and a clear list of practices to avoid. Require any rules violation to be approved by the chief architect or the technical manager or both.

Conclusion

The number of excellent object-oriented software engineers in the market remains small compared with the overall population of programmers. The more you strengthen your skills and talents in this area, the more valuable you will become to your company—and to any other that might want you.

References

Meyers, Scott. *Effective C++*. Reading, Mass.: Addison-Wesley, 1992.

Taligent, Inc. *Taligent's Guide to Designing Programs*. Reading, Mass.: Addison-Wesley, 1994.

CHAPTER 7:

CLASS AND OBJECT PITFALLS

The sublime and the ridiculous are often so nearly related, that it is difficult to class them separately. One step above the sublime, makes the ridiculous; and one step above the ridiculous, makes the sublime again.

—Tom Paine (1795)

I learned Pascal in 1980 while working at the Lunar and Planetary Institute. The high-level language that I had previously used most heavily—and exclusively since leaving college—was FORTRAN. Arrays were all that FORTRAN had for data structures, and I was very, very good at building whatever data structures I needed from arrays. But Pascal offered arrays and records and sets and strings, and I suddenly felt at a bit of a loss. I would construct a data structure one way, and then wonder whether there was a better way. As the months went by, I became more and more confident and skilled at creating the right Pascal data structures for a given problem.

Designing classes and objects is much the same. If you're new at it, you may feel a bit awkward or even lost at first. Or you may rush ahead, thinking that everything is going just swell, until you suddenly run into problems that make you rethink your implementation. Use the following collection of pitfalls as a checklist to evaluate the objects you're creating, but be sure to use them on a regular basis—many of these pitfalls can creep up on you.

If you're a technical manager, you can use these pitfalls as a guideline to help you evaluate the design and implementation produced by your developers, or simply to help you ask the developers penetrating (and possibly uncomfortable) questions. In either case, a knowledge of these pitfalls should help to improve the quality of object design and implementation.

Pitfall 7.1: Confusing is-a, has-a, and is-implemented-using Relationships.

There are three basic relationships between object classes: **is-a**, **has-a**, and **is-implemented-using**. Failing to understand these relationships can lead to poor class and hierarchy design, not to mention serious problems down the road.

The **is-a** relationship reflects going from a general class of objects to a specialized class (or subclass). We deal with this relationship in the real world: For example, a lizard **is-a** reptile, a reptile **is-a(n)** animal, an animal **is-a** life form. The **is-a** relationship is at the core of the inheritance concept in object-oriented development: A derived or subclass **is-a** base or superclass, with whatever specialization is desired. Note that there is an explicit direction: Although every lizard **is-a** reptile, it is not true that every reptile **is-a** lizard. This may seem like an obvious error, but it's not uncommon for a developer to make Ellipse a subclass of Circle instead of the other way around.

The **has-a** relationship reflects a whole-component relationship: A car **has-a** engine, a car **has-a** door(s), a car **has-a** tire(s). This relationship is not unique to OOD. It's found in a wide variety of languages and approaches. Novice object-oriented developers sometimes use inheritance to implement **has-a**, such as making Car a subclass of Engine. Instead, they should use data members so that a Car object has a data member that points to an Engine object.

The **is-implemented-using** relationship falls between the two. For example, a list of contacts **is-implemented-using** a notebook. The relationship is neither inheritance nor component; I might use several different things to implement my list of contacts. Even developers with experience in OOD may fall into the mistake of using inheritance. For example, they may derive the class ContactList from Notebook rather than having ContactList own a Notebook as a data member.

Symptoms   Trouble mapping class hierarchy to problem space; constant struggles with classes; constant rearranging of hierarchy.

Consequences   Poor hierarchy design; unnecessary complexity in project; loss of OOD benefits.

Detection   Sit down with your class hierarchy. For each Base-Derived class pair, where Derived is a subclass of Base, see whether it's true that Derived always **is-a** Base but false that Base always **is-a** Derived. If any test fails, then you've got confusion in your class hierarchy.

(However, if Derived doesn't inherit or make public Base's interface, there might not be an **is-a** relationship; see the next pitfall.)

Extraction   Having detected a problem, check first to identify your error. Is it reversal of an **is-a** relationship, substitution of **is-a** for **has-a,** or substitution of **is-a** for **is-implemented-using**? Adjust the class hierarchy and data members accordingly, using the guidelines given above. That sounds easy, but it can actually wreak havoc with your project. Be prepared for some real struggles, especially if you've been using archived object streams to save out and read in object instances.

Prevention   Set guidelines for creating class hierarchies. For each class to be defined, use the descriptions above to determine its relationship with existing classes. This problem is far easier to avoid than to correct.

Pitfall 7.2: Confusing interface inheritance with implementation inheritance.

A derived class generally inherits three things from its base class: its interface (or protocol), which is the set of methods visible to other classes; its data members; and its implementation of any declared methods. Inheritance of data members is usually straightforward (except, of course, in cases of multiple inheritance, but we'll leave that discussion to language-specific books). Because many object-oriented programming languages (OOPLs) support both private and public interface portions and because some support public vs. private derivation, it's important to distinguish between interface inheritance and implementation inheritance.

Given that Derived is a subclass of Base, then Derived inherits Base's interface if Derived provides (makes public) each method provided (made public) by Base. Generally speaking, public interface inheritance means that Derived **is-a** Base. **Protected** or **private interface** inheritance usually means that Derived **is-implemented-using** Base, and you may wish to consider making an instance of Base a data member of Derived instead of making it Derived's superclass.

Given that Derived is a subclass of Base, then Derived inherits Base's implementation of a given method if Derived does not provide its own implementation of that method. For the case of that method, Derived behaves just like Base—unless, of course, the method calls other methods for which Derived provided its own implementation. For a given method, Derived may choose to provide its own implementation, by either replacing or extending Base's implementation; however, note that the OOPL you're using may imply or enforce restrictions. (For example, it's good practice in C++ to override only virtual functions and to assume that nonvirtual functions are not to be overridden.)

You face the following possible combinations for each method inherited by Derived from Base:

- Public interface (can be called by other classes):
- Base's implementation: Strong **is-a** relationship. If most methods are like this, then Derived might be folded back into Base.
- Derived's implementation extends Base's implementation: Classic **is-a** relationship, reflecting that Derived is a specialization of Base.

- Derived's implementation replaces Base's implementation: If Base's implementation is significant, this can signal a weakening **is-a** relationship; otherwise, it is a classic **is-a** relationship, especially if Base's implementation is empty.
- Protected interface (can be called only by Derived and its subclasses): Weak **is-a** relationship; implies more of an **is-implemented-using** relationship.
- Private interface (cannot be called directly by Derived): Strong **is-implemented-using** relationship.

Symptoms   Trouble mapping class hierarchy to problem space; constant struggles with classes; constant rearranging of hierarchy.

Consequences   Poor hierarchy design; unnecessary complexity in project; loss of OOD benefits.

Detection   For each base-derived class pair, go through each method in Base and categorize the interface and implementation inheritance expressed in Derived. Note what is actually happening as opposed to what the class design intends. It may also help to see whether there is confusion between **is-a**, **has-a**, and **is-implemented-using** relationships (see Pitfall 7.1).

Extraction   Set up the interface and implementation inheritance according to the class design. This may involve changes to the hierarchy itself, but that's less likely than with the previous pitfall.

Prevention   Set clear guidelines for how methods should be exported and inherited or overridden. These may well be language-specific, because each OOPL has differences in what is allowed and what is supposed to be done.

Pitfall 7.3: Using inheritance badly.

Believe it or not, not everyone involved in object-oriented development considers inheritance an important part of OOD. Susan Lily raised the question, "Is inheritance dangerous?" George Bosworth opined, "In my view, inheritance is primarily a hack to make programmers more productive—an elegant and beautiful hack, and thus very elegant". Some firms (such as Microsoft) deny that inheritance is necessary to call something object-oriented (such as Microsoft's OLE 2.0).

So what are the problems with inheritance? Several pitfalls have been outlined in the previous two sections (7.1, 7.2), but there are others. These include:

- **Using inheritance to violate encapsulation**. Because creating a subclass may give you direct access to all instance variables and lets you override or extend method implementations, you can hack on the "guts" of a given class just by subclassing it. You may do this to accomplish a task that by rights should be done in a cleaner, more stable fashion.

- **Using multiple inheritance (MI) to invert the** is-a **relationship.** By combining two or more classes, you can create a more general class from two specific ones; the classic example is to combine Dog and Cat to form Animal. This may seem silly to you, but it has actually been done.

- **Using multiple inheritance at all.** This remains a topic of some controversy within the object development community. Some people are opposed to all use of MI; others (including me) like the idea of using a single base class and multiple mixin classes; still others want multiple base classes. Just be aware that MI can get you into a lot of trouble and should be considered a potential pitfall.

These and similar misuses of inheritance may seem to have some short-term value, but they will usually come back to haunt you in the end.

Symptoms   Trouble mapping class hierarchy to problem space; constant struggles with classes; constant rearranging of hierarchy.

Consequences   Low rate of reuse; product instability; high support and maintenance costs; little architectural flexibility.

Detection   Use the detection methods in Pitfalls 7.1 and 7.2: class and hierarchy design reviews. That process should flush out any misuse or poor use of inheritance.

Extraction   If possible, clean up things—eliminate the poor use of inheritance—before project completion. Otherwise, complete the project and go on to **Prevention**.

Prevention   Establish standards and guidelines for how inheritance is used. Enforce by periodically holding class and hierarchy design reviews.

Pitfall 7.4: Having base classes do too much or too little.

A base class is intended to be the foundation for derived classes. In this role it establishes the common behavior, which derived classes then inherit, build on, or override. Base classes are the key to many of the software reuse benefits of object-oriented development.

There are two general categories: abstract base classes and concrete base classes. Abstract base classes aren't meant to be instantiated; in some object-oriented programming languages, you can't instantiate them. A concrete base class can and should be instantiated; if it never is, then it should be considered an abstract base class.

When is a base class doing too little? First, when the base class has few or no public methods. Any public derivation implies inheritance of interface; if there's no interface to be inherited, then there's little reason for the base class to exist. The base class may be a placeholder, something created early in the project as a "good idea" that was never used or deleted.

The second clue is that when the public methods in the base class are mostly empty so that there is little implementation inheritance. This usually reflects the developer's desire to establish a protocol, but to let each derived class implement it a different way. Lack of inherited implementation can weaken the **is-a** relationship implicit in the public interface inheritance.

Third, you are underusing base classes if there is a lot of similar or duplicate code in its derived classes. This implies a common functionality which should be generalized and moved up into the base class.

When is a base class doing too much? When it offers an implementation of a given method, but most or all derived classes override that method. This suggests either a weakness in the **is-a** relationship between the base and derived classes or a need to redesign the base class itself.

Symptoms   For base classes doing too little: no apparent generalization or code reuse. For those doing too much: ignored implementations.

Consequences   Extra time spent on derived classes; limited reusability of base classes because of extra work required to create a derived class.

Detection   Use the tests given above: Few or no public methods; public methods lack implementations; lots of similar or duplicate code in derived classes; most or all derived classes override a given method.

Extraction   This problem is often easy to fix. It usually involves only a rebalancing of functionality between the base class and its derived classes. If most or all of the base class's public methods are empty, you might consider making the base class a mixin class (in C++) or a protocol (in Objective-C).

Prevention   Set guidelines to create base and derived classes and then see that they're followed. Do periodic design and code reviews of base and derived classes (as per **Detection,** above) to see whether problems are creeping in.

Pitfall 7.5: Not preserving base class invariants.

As noted in Pitfall 6.2, a given class has many invariants: implementation details that embody and define its behavior and nature. They can include assumed preconditions and resulting postconditions for each method; ranges and combinations of acceptable values for incoming parameters; all possible valid states for a given object class or instance and the circumstances under which it should or should not assume each; all system consequences; constraints on timing and circumstances when a given method can be called; and behavior associated with each state.

To understand these invariants may require significant analysis of the class. They certainly aren't all obvious or even discernible from the language-level interface for a class, and they may not be obvious from the implementation source code.

Because of this, programmers may derive a subclass from a base class without fully understanding all that's being (or should be) inherited. But when optimum inheritance fails to happen, the developers also fail to preserve the relationship implied by that inheritance.

The flip side happens when we change the invariants for a given base class. If we take no further actions, we may break the invariants for any derived classes.

Symptoms   Inconsistencies in object behavior. Hierarchy problems.

Consequences   Weakening of the inheritance relationship, be it **is-a** or **is-implemented-using**. Possible late bugs and schedule slip on shipment.

Detection   It will take a careful code and design review of the base class and any derived classes to identify the invariants in the base class and determine whether each derived class properly preserves those invariants. But this review is necessary to identify this pitfall.

Extraction   After performing **Detection**, make the appropriate repairs to the derived classes and to other parts of the project that depend on the old (erroneous) behavior of the derived classes.

Prevention   Establish an "invariants" document for each object class. Use it to document all invariants for that class. Update the document as changes are made to the class.

Before creating a subclass, the architect or engineer should review invariants document of the base class to ensure preservation. The engineer then creates an invariants document for the new subclass, noting any differences in invariants and documenting any new ones.

When changes are made to a base class, its invariants document should be updated (if necessary). Also, all derived classes should be reexamined for possible changes to their invariants.

Pitfall 7.6: Converting non-object code straight into objects.

Developers with no object-oriented experience are used to using (and often merging) two different approaches to program organization: data-oriented and process-oriented practices. Data orientation is conducted by creating data structures, particularly records or structs. Process orientation is performed by creating sets of functions or subroutines, often collected into modules. Object-oriented development adopts a natural combination of these two approaches. This technique involves defining data fields and the processes to manipulate them.

Developers new to OOD sometimes extend their former approaches to OOD in a one-sided fashion. For example, they may take a data structure, turn it into a class, define methods to access (set and get) the data fields, and leave it at that. The resulting class is little more than a cumbersome version of the original data structure, with no intelligence or behavior built into it.

On the process side, developers may take a set of functions and turn them into methods in a single class, possibly with few or no data members. The class doesn't model or reflect an object in the problem space; it just becomes another form of module, unit, or library.

This problem often shows up when existing non-OO code is being converted to an object-oriented design. But it may also occur if developers with little OOD experience are asked to design objects on their own.

Symptoms   Objects that look suspiciously like modules, libraries, data structures, or other non-OOD code or data constructs.

Consequences Poor class design; poor hierarchy design; poor mapping to problem domain.

Detection   If a class has well-defined data members but no real functionality besides accessing those members, you may have a problem. If a class has lots of methods that have little bearing on the data members, especially if the data members themselves are few or nonexistent, you have a problem.

Extraction   Review each suspect class, and, while you're at it, review the whole class hierarchy. You can often clean up data-centric classes by adding appropriate methods, which may well be found in (or deduced from) other classes. Process-centric classes should be broken up and their functionality distributed among the relevant classes.

Prevention   Do a good job of project design and architecture, and conduct careful review of all proposed classes.

Pitfall 7.7: Letting objects become bloated.

A bloated object is one with too many data members and methods or one that eats up too many pages when printed out. You may note that "too many" is in the eye of the beholder—arguments still remain from the 1970s about how long a function or subroutine should be—and you're exactly right. When the developers who must extend, correct, debug, and use an object find it increasingly difficult to manage the object's complexity, then it is probably bloated.

An object class becomes bloated for several reasons. It may be attempting too much; for example, a single object may implement an entire text system. It may have started out small and grown as more and more methods, data members, and code were added. It may be a base class that is attempting to do too much for all its derived classes. For that matter, it may be attempting to handle too many different situations, lumping what should be several derived classes into a single class.

Symptoms   Large source code files; long lists of data members and methods; difficulties in understanding and debugging certain classes.

Consequences   Increased program complexity; persistent bugs; unpredictable behavior; large memory footprint.

Detection   Count the number of data members, methods, and lines of code for each object class. Use these values to create three different sorted lists (highest to lowest) based on each of the values. For each list, do a code and design review for the first several classes on it.

Extraction   Object bloat is usually reduced by successive application of **is-a, has-a,** and **is-implemented-using** relationships. Here are steps to consider to trim a bloated object, depending on what makes the most sense in the context of your problem and design:

- Migrate some of the code into an existing base class (**is-a**).
- Split the object into a base class and one or more derived classes (**is-a**).
- Split the object into a container class and one or more component classes, so that the container class has data members that are instances of the component classes (**has-a**).
- Extract the data manipulation implementation of the object into a separate class and make that a data member of the original class (**is-implemented-using**).

Prevention   During class and hierarchy design, ask yourself repeatedly whether a given class runs the danger of becoming bloated. Keep in mind the factors that lead to object bloat. As development proceeds, use the **Detection** and **Extraction** methods on a regular basis to check for bloat-by-accretion.

Pitfall 7.8: Letting objects ooze.

The touted benefits of object-oriented development include better management of complexity, code reuse, and greater robustness. One concept leading to these benefits is encapsulation: hiding implementation behind a clean, intelligent interface. A good visual image for a well-designed object class is of a hard, curved, solid shape—a capsule, if you will—with several access ports that require standard connectors.

Unfortunately, our objects are not always that clean and solid. Indeed, at times they bear a greater resemblance to an amorphous organic mass in a laboratory, floating in liquid, with tubes, wires, and probes running into it at various points. Kind of disgusting, isn't it? It's also a real pain to maintain, extend, and correct; we end up rearranging existing wires and tubes—or adding new ones.

There are several factors behind oozing objects, including:

- Encapsulation failure: making the internal implementation of the object visible to other classes. "Visible" can be read in a literal sense—allowing access to data members and methods that should be private—and in a conceptual sense: letting other classes depend on implementation details and side effects.
- Object bloat (see previous pitfall). The more bloated an object is, the more likely it is to ooze.
- Complex interface design: Interface complexity is measured by the number of methods offered, the average number of parameters per method, the average number of methods that must be called to carry out a given operation, and the degree of interdependency between method calls.
- Poor class and hierarchy design: Confusion of **is-a**, **has-a**, and **is-implemented-using** relationships can lead to oozing objects.

Symptoms   Difficulties debugging a given object class; a tendency for changes in that class to break the project; a tendency for developers to avoid working on that class.

Consequences   Poor management of complexity; persistent bugs; fragile and unstable code; low rate of reuse.

Detection   If you suspect an object class of oozing (or threatening to), evaluate the four factors given above as they apply to that class. If one or more factors are present, then there's a good chance that your object is beginning to ooze.

Extraction

Detecting an oozing object is usually easier than cleaning it up. But you can do it by addressing each of the problem areas:

- Seal encapsulation better by hiding implementation details and assumptions. If you're having a hard time doing this, there may be other, more serious flaws in your class, hierarchy, and project design.

- Cure object bloat by the methods described in the previous pitfall. Reduce interface complexity through redesign and refactoring. Clarify **is-a**, **has-a**, and **is-implemented-using** relationships as described in the earlier pitfall.

Prevention

As with bloated objects, you can prevent oozing objects by carefully thinking and planning throughout the initial design and architecture phases, by establishing guidelines for class design, and by implementing a regular program of code hygiene.

Pitfall 7.9: Creating Swiss Army knife objects.

A Swiss Army™ knife is a wonderful gadget to keep in your pocket. Depending on the selection of blades and attachments on your particular model, you can carve wood, scale a fish, clip your toenails, open a can of beans, remove a cork, or tighten screws. In most cases, the knife doesn't perform any given task as well as a single tool does that's designed specifically for that same task. But it's a lot more convenient than lugging around the assortment of tools necessary to perform all the same tasks. Just ask MacGyver.

Some developers succumb to the temptation to create objects that begin to resemble Swiss Army knives. They start out with a well-designed object class, much like a plain knife. Then they need a simple function, perhaps one loosely related to the class. Rather than create a new object class or reconsider their existing design, they add a method to the class. This turns out to be so easy—and so much easier than introducing changes in the class hierarchy—that they do it again and again, often for functions with an ever-more-tenuous connection to the class.

This habit may seem innocuous, but the consequences can come back to haunt you. By building Swiss Army knife objects, you build a lot of dependencies on this class that have nothing to do with the class's original intent and design. Later in development, you may find yourself needing to change the class and hierarchy design, which may involve substantially modifying or even eliminating this class or perhaps changing its visibility or scope. If you have introduced dependencies on this class that have nothing to do with its purpose you will have to find a way to break or maintain those dependencies.

Symptoms An object class that starts handling a variety of loosely connected (or unconnected) functions.

Consequences Class dependencies unrelated to the problem space or class design.

Detection Write a brief summary of what a class is supposed to represent and how it maps into the original problem space. Then go through all the methods in the class and evaluate how well each relates to the original intent; Give it a rating of 0 (not at all) to 4 (absolutely). Any methods with a rating of 2 or less are an indication that you're starting to drift into this pitfall.

Extraction Review all the methods you rated 2 or less during the **Detection** exercise and consider where these methods should be located. Some may be better placed (have a higher rating) in other object classes. Others should be folded into the classes that call them. Still others should be collected into a new object class.

Prevention Before adding any method to a new or existing class, perform the rating method described in **Detection**. If you get a value of 2 or less, reconsider what you're doing.

Pitfall 7.10: Creating hyperspaghetti objects and subsystems.

We tend to think of "spaghetti code" as going out of style during the late 1970s with the advent of structured programming and the trend against using goto statements. By and large, it has vanished. It is ironic that object-oriented development, of all things, would reintroduce a kind of "hyperspaghetti code" pitfall.

In functional decomposition—process-oriented software design—you establish a direct, tight flow of execution. By following proper structured programming techniques, you get clear, predictable, easy-to-follow behavior. Most software engineers are used to this process and its results and take both for granted. When they start OOD, they often fall into the assumption that as long as they build well-designed objects and the objects call themselves and other objects through methods, the result is clean flow of execution and predictable behavior.

That's not the case. In functional decomposition, any subroutine can, in theory, call any other visible subroutine; but the very process of functional decomposition ensures a proper flow of execution to avert problems. In OOD, any object can, in theory, call any other visible object and often does. Flow-of-execution design in OOD is far more tedious and difficult than in functional decomposition; OO developers often avoid it, and new ones might not even realize they have to worry about it. Add to that equation issues of inheritance execution and the event-driven environment in which most OOD is done, and you have the makings of a real mess.

Symptoms   Unpredictable behavior of objects; persistent bugs; low rate of code reuse.

Consequences   Unpredictable behavior of objects; persistent bugs; low rate of code reuse.

Detection   When symptoms appear, sit down with the engineers involved and start tracing flow of execution. Pick a starting point triggered by a repeatable event, such as a mouse click or keystroke. Step through the code using a debugger, but take notes about the actual flow of execution. Note any surprises along the way. If you find yourself lost, tired, out of paper, or suffering a headache, you've probably got a real problem.

Extraction   It's not easy. It will probably involve serious rethinking and redesign of object relationships and interactions; after all, you got there in the first place while trying to do your best to get the job done. You may have to live with the current situation until the project is finished and then look for an opportunity to revamp and rearchitect in the next release.

Prevention Force yourself and all other developers to do flow-of-execution design and analysis in advance. It's tedious, so expect resistance from yourself and your developers. It takes time, so expect resistance from upper management.

Conclusion

Class and object design is an art and a skill that comes with time, thought, learning, practice, and experience. Class and object implementation is a science, based on careful following of canonical forms, coding standards, pre and postconditions, and other aspects of software engineering. By combining these factors, you can create classes that are:

- logical
- relevant
- lightweight
- subclassable
- portable
- loosely coupled
- resuable

As you focus on these goals, you can avoid most of the pitfalls described in this chapter.

References

Bosworth, George. "Objects, not classes, are the issues." *Object Magazine*, 2(4), Nov/Dec 1992.

Lily, Susan. "Is object-oriented programming harmful?" *Object Magazine*, 3(2), Jul/Aug 1992.

CHAPTER 8:
CODING PITFALLS

A perfect method should not only be an efficient one, as respects the accomplishment of the objects for which it is designed, but should in all its parts and processes manifest a certain unity and harmony.

—George Boole, *An Investigation of the Laws of Thought*

Because coding pitfalls are often tied to a language, I wondered whether to include this chapter at all, or to simply leave this topic to language-specific books. However, thought and research make it clear that some general coding pitfalls tend to occur in object-oriented development. Here are a few for your consideration.

Pitfall 8.1: Copying objects.

"Copying objects" as a pitfall may seem a bit broad and dramatic, but that's how I wanted it. You take risks when you create a copy of an object or make an assignment. The risks and issues will vary among languages, and you should look to see which apply for the languages you use.

Issue Number 1: bitwise copy vs. member copy. When one object is assigned to another, is a bit-by-bit (or byte-by-byte) copy made, or are copies and assignments done for each instance variable (data member)? This may not seem to make a difference, but it does; those members may be objects themselves and raise the same issue for each one.

Issue Number 2: shallow copy vs. deep copy. When a member copy is done, is it shallow (actual values of each member are copied) or deep (object instances are subjected to a deep copy of their own)? Some languages (such as Smalltalk) offer explicit operators to distinguish between the two; others require you to define your own.

Issue Number 3: copying vs. assignment vs. initialization. Different results may happen when you copy an object (such as passing it by value to a method), when you assign one object to another, and when you create a new object with initial values.

Issue Number 4: slicing objects. In some languages, most notably C++, it is possible to do an upcast—assign an instance of a derived class to an instance of one of its base classes. By doing so, you may lose all the data members not declared in that base class; this is known as **slicing**. Besides losing data, you can lose objects, creating a memory leak if any of those members had pointers to other objects.

Issue Number 5: working on a copy of an object instead of on the object itself (or vice versa). When you pass an object to a method, that object gets passed along (generally speaking) in one of two ways: Either the object itself (or a reference to it) is passed it, or a copy of the object is made. If you're not careful, you may find yourself getting one when you expect the other. Furthermore, if a copy is created, you need to know whether it received its values via copying (bitwise? member? shallow? deep?), assignment, or initialization.

In short, there are many ways for things to go wrong or objects to behave unexpectedly any time an object is copied.

Symptoms   They vary based on the error and the language. Look for bugs where operations meant for a given object don't seem to occur or seem to be happening to other objects.

Consequences   Nasty, persistent bugs. Instability and unreliability.

Detection   Use the itemized issues above to discover how things operate in your language and in your project.

Extraction   Create separate and distinct methods and functions to handle all the means of copying: bitwise, shallow member, deep member, assignment, initialization. Test them thoroughly to ensure that they behave as expected. Then phase them into your code.

Prevention   Before coding, set up the methods and functions described in **Extraction.** If the members must be defined for each new class, make them part of a rigorous canonical class format that must be used for every class.

Pitfall 8.2: Testing objects for equality and identity.

This is another classic problem: What defines two objects of the same class as being equal? Are they equal only if they are indeed the same object—that is, you have two pointers to the same chunk of memory that the object occupies? Are the two objects equal if all their instance variables (data members) have the same values? Is that a "shallow" comparison (member values only) or a "deep" comparison (recursive through other objects pointed to)? Or are the objects equal based on criteria specific to the class itself?

Conversely, how do you uniquely identify a given object? During execution, reliance is often placed on either symbol names (for object variables) or memory addresses (for pointers). But when you have to deal with object identification across networks or object persistence between execution sessions, the problem of identity becomes more difficult.

Symptoms	Unexpected failure of equality or identity tests.
Consequences	Bugs.
Detection	Set up small test cases and check the results.
Extraction	Introduce or begin to use explicit methods or functions to test equality and establish identity.
Prevention	Create explicit methods or functions to test equality and establish identity. Make them standard (again, part of the canonical class form, when applicable) and enforce their use.

Pitfall 8.3: Not keeping track of objects.

Objects come and go frequently during the course of program execution. They form intricate and complex relationships with each other. In the shuffle, two things can happen to an object:

1. Two or more objects can compete for (or simply assume) ownership and control.
2. All other objects can forget about it.

Let's take the first case. Both Object A and Object B have pointers to Object Q, and both assume that they have ownership. A completes its work with Q and frees it. B attempts to perform work with Q. Boom! This is known as a **stale,** or **dangling, reference.**

Let's take the second case. Again, Objects A and B have pointers to Object Q, but neither A nor B assumes ownership. A finishes with Q and zeros out its pointer to Q. B does the same thing. Neither has any way to find Q and release its memory, so Q just sits in the memory pool, taking up space. This is known as a **memory leak.**

Consider this alternative second case: A and B each attempt to free Q. Thanks to garbage collection or reference counting (see **Prevention**), Q is safely freed at the right time. But Q was actually supposed to stick around!

Symptoms   Program crashes. Lost data. Increased memory consumption during execution.

Consequences   See **Symptoms**.

Detection   The stale references are pretty easy to detect; they tend to flush themselves out. Memory leaks usually require the use of a system or debugging utility to monitor memory consumption or make explicit tests for memory leaks.

Extraction   See **Prevention**.

Prevention   This pitfall has two fundamental issues. The first issue is garbage collection, which refers to freeing previously allocated memory that is no longer needed. Some languages provide this automatically, but others (including C++) do not. If your language doesn't provide garbage collection, then you have two choices. You can attempt to program around it, trying to ensure that you will never, ever have a stale reference or a memory leak. Or you can implement some form of **reference counting.**

Here, in simple terms, is how reference counting works. Each object maintains a count of the number of references to it. Each time another object establishes a reference to the object, the count increases by one. Each time another object abandons a reference, the count is decremented. If the count reaches its initial value (say, 0), the object has no more references to it and can be safely freed. The catch is that you have to implement all this, including making sure that each and every relevant object follows proper procedure.

The second issue is that of **ownership** of a given object. Garbage collection or reference counting aside, this concept is useful for managing an object's creation and destruction. For example, a given object (Q) is created by its owner, which is another object (A). Only A can free Q; all other objects can refer to Q, but have to recognize that A can get rid of Q at any time. If A wishes to hand ownership of Q to another object (B), A **orphans** Q and B **adopts** Q.

By incorporating the concept and practices of ownership into your object design and implementation along with implementing garbage collection or reference counting to handle memory recycling, you stand a much higher chance of keeping track of the objects you wish to and getting rid of those slated for destruction.

Pitfall 8.4: Consuming memory inadvertently.

Pitfall 8.3 talked about a memory leak caused by having all objects clear their references to a given object Q without that object actually being freed. That is one way in which your object-oriented program can eat up memory without realizing it, but there are others.

A second memory leak scenario can occur through object composition (**has-a**) relationships. You define an object, SomeThing, with several instance variables (data members). Most of these instance variables point to other object instances or to lists of object instances. But each instance variable has its own set of **has-a** relationships or chunks of memory to allocate for data, and so on, and so forth. Before you know it, each instance of SomeThing allocates thousands, tens of thousands, or even hundreds of thousands of bytes of memory. Even on systems with true virtual memory, allocations of that degree can eat up swap space and can slow performance.

A third way memory is gobbled is by object proliferation. You may define a fairly lightweight object, with a size measured in the tens of bytes. But your application architecture may allocate tens of thousands of these small objects. Again, your system must suddenly deal with lots of memory getting eaten up.

Yet another way this pitfall can occur is if you have methods set up to do a pass-by-value, which requires a copy to be made of each object passed in. This is no problem if the object is light, but if it's sized like SomeThing, you can find a sudden (and hidden) demand for memory. The problem is worse if several pass-by-value calls exist within a calling chain, which requires that a new object copy be made for each call in the chain.

Symptoms   Out-of-memory errors, large swapfiles, slow performance, disk swapping.

Consequences   Poor performance, large memory or disk requirements.

Detection   Some systems or environments have developer utilities (bundled or available from third parties) to check memory allocation. Lacking that, you can run your own tests, especially if memory allocation and object creation are done through one or more standard methods or functions.

Extraction   For this pitfall, awareness is 90 percent of the solution. If you know where the memory is going, then you can decide what, if any, action to take: Cutting down on object size or object count, passing objects in by reference, or other remedies.

Prevention   Build in your own methods and functions for object creation and allocation. Set these before programming, to monitor memory allocated. Use them to look for big objects, large numbers of objects, or any uncomfortable combination of both.

Pitfall 8.5: Confusing switch statements and polymorphism.

There is an often-quoted rule of thumb in object-oriented development that any time you see a **switch (case)** statement or its equivalent in **if/then/else** statements, it means that someone didn't use polymorphism properly. I believe that this rule is an oversimplification—well intentioned, but oversimplified nevertheless. Let's look at some specific situations and what they might mean.

Case Number 1: selecting on the object class. Suppose you have code that tests the class type of a given Object Q and takes action based on the result: **If (class == Circle) then do X1, else if (class == Square) then do X2, else<** and so on. This code is a likely candidate for polymorphism; there should be some method **doX** that does the proper thing for each class (**X1** for Circle objects, **X2** for **Square** objects, and so on).

Case Number 2: selecting on an object attribute outside the object instance. In this case, you query the object Q for an attribute, then take action based on the result: **if(color == blue) then do C1, else if (color == red), then do C2, else<** and so on. If C1, C2, and the others are methods of Q, then again this is probably a candidate for polymorphism. If, on the other hand, C1 and the rest are chunks of code or methods for other objects (including the calling one), then it is less clear that these should be somehow moved into Q's class.

Case Number 3: selecting on an object attribute within the object instance. Suppose that it is Q that, inside its own method, is interrogating an attribute of itself and taking action based on the result: **if(color == blue) then do** and so on. This is when the generalization gets dangerous. Some programmers would argue that there should be subclasses of Q's class for each color; this may seem ridiculous, but if we change color to shape (triangle, square, circle) then you may find yourself in agreement.

Case Number 4: deriving subclasses based on a discrete attribute. Suppose you have a base class, Shape, with subclasses for Circle, Square, Triangle, and so on. Determine the real differences among these subclasses and between each subclass and the base class. You may be better off collapsing them to a single subclass.

The core of the tension here seems to be when classes have attributes that can be expressed in enumerated types. We wouldn't consider having subclasses based on weight, because of the range of values and the fine gradations; yet we assume other, more distinct values or attributes to be different.

Symptoms   Too many **switch** statements. Or, in contrast, too many sibling-derived classes based on a given attribute or aspect.

Consequences Poor design. Less flexibility and generality. Less reuse.

Detection   Examine the code for **switch** statement equivalents. Examine the class hierarchy for similar siblings.

Extraction   Make the proper conversion (going from a **switch** statement to polymorphism or collapsing several classes into a single class).

Prevention   Establish design and implementation guidelines before beginning coding. Do periodic **Detection** and **Extraction** checks.

Conclusions

The problems and procedures discussed in this chapter may not seem like much, but if you can master these coding pitfalls and avoid them in your own implementation, you will have greatly improved your code's quality and reliability.

CHAPTER 9:

QUALITY ASSURANCE PITFALLS

Now good my lord, let there be some more test made of my mettle before so
noble and so great a figure be stamp'd upon it.

—William Shakespeare, Measure for Measure, Act 1, Scene 1

For all the hoopla over quality during the last few years, software quality assurance remains a poor cousin in many companies and organizations. SQA involves testing software both for compliance with specification and for bugs, as well as providing technical support after the software is delivered. These jobs are difficult to do well, requiring skill, training, and experience, but the attitude taken by upper management is often that warm bodies pulled off the street and paid minimum wage can do the job well. As the saying goes, you get what you pay for.

For reasons outlined in this chapter, the challenge is even greater with object-oriented development. The opportunity is also greater. An SQA group trained in testing object components can be a tremendous force for ensuring quality of design and implementation as the software is being built, instead of having to wait until everything is finished before becoming involved. As noted in this chapter, technical managers would do well to think of OOD as consisting primarily of two activities—design and testing—with a thin sliver of implementation in between.

Pitfall 9.1: Forgetting the combinatorial explosion.

Object-oriented development conveys a sense of freedom. It conjures a picture of a sea of objects floating in cyberspace and sending messages back and forth. There's even a certain egalitarianism in it, with all the objects talking freely to one another. But within that freedom lurks a danger, one that eerily parallels the classic communication problem of large software teams: The number of possible message links among objects increases geometrically as the number of objects increases. Given 10 objects that can send messages to each other and recognizing that Object A sending a message to Object B is quite different from B sending a message to A, you end up with $N*(N-1)$, or 90, possible links. For 100 objects, that's 9,900 message links, and so on.

But wait! It gets worse. There can be M different message links from Object A to Object B, where M represents the number of methods belonging to B that A can call. If you sum that for each sender-receiver object pair, the $N*(N-1)$ value now becomes merely the lower bound. The upper bound is now $S*(N-1)$, where S is the sum total of all accessible methods found in the N objects. Just for fun, let's assume an average of 8 methods per object class. For 10 objects, the upper bound of message links is now 720, and the upper bound for 100 objects approaches 80,000 distinct message links.

On top of this, you also must deal with the possible ranges of parameter values being passed among objects for a specific method call, as well as the state of the receiving object when the method call is made. This pushes the number of distinct message links into the astronomical ranges. Some folding and collapsing does occur—not all objects talk to all other objects, not all methods are available to all objects, and so on—but even after that factoring, the numbers remain very, very high. And you have to make sure all this works correctly.

Symptoms Difficulties in predicting behavior, tracking down bugs, and making things work just right.

Consequences Instability; unpredictable behavior; persistent bugs; constant schedule slips.

Detection Do the math. To make things easier, build into your project trace code that logs into a file the source object, destination object, method, and parameter values every time a message is sent from one object to another. Turn it on, use your application, turn it off. Look at the log file.

Extraction Find ways to reduce the combinatorial factors. This process may not be easy or even possible, given your current design, but try it anyway. Here are the factors to work on:

- Work to make objects less visible to each other.
- For every sender-receiver object pair, A->B, do the following:
  - Reduce the number of different messages that A sends to B.
  - Reduce the number of times A calls a given method of B.
  - Reduce the range of parameter values A sends to B for a given method.
- For each method M of a given receiver object B, do the following:
  - Where possible, make M's behavior more state-invariant with regard to B; make the consequences of calling M less dependent or even independent of B's state at the time of the call.
  - Work to make M's behavior more source-invariant—independent or less dependent on the object calling M.
  - Do proper conditioning of input parameters to reduce the number of possible outcomes (including new states for B).
- For each sender Object A, sending method M to Object B, do the following:
  - Ensure that B is in the proper state to receive M.
  - Condition any parameters being passed to M to ensure that they fall within legal and desirable bounds.

The more you can reduce these factors, the more stable and predictable your code will be.

Prevention Use the techniques described in **Extraction** as you design the class hierarchy and the project. Use white box testing (described in Pitfall 9.2), automated where possible, to drive a class or subsystem through the full range of method calls.

Pitfall 9.2: Neglecting component testing.

Given the potential complexity of object-oriented systems, as described in Pitfall 9.1, classic SQA testing procedures probably won't be adequate for an object-oriented project of any size. Even with carefully written test scripts—and few software development groups prepare careful test scripts—your testing will still be hit-and-miss for any application that has an object complexity above a certain threshold.

One solution is to implement component testing. This involves methodically testing components—individual objects or object subsystems—independently of the project, to ensure correct and predictable behavior. Component testing has two basic types. **White box testing** is done by someone who has access to the source code of the component and who can insert commands to trace execution, monitor and log values, and cause execution to stop (typically to drop into a debugger) if illegal or nonsensical values are passed in or if the object gets into an invalid or suspect state. White box testing should be done by someone other than the engineer responsible for the component and preferably by someone not on the development team.

Black box testing is done by someone who has access to a compiled copy of the component and documentation about the component's interface. The tester writes test objects that try to make all possible calls to the component; the tester notes the results of each attempt. This may seem superfluous if white box testing is done, but black box testing has benefits above and beyond simply testing for errors.

Symptoms   Persistent instability and bugs in certain subsystems and components.

Consequences   Instability, unpredictable behavior, persistent bugs, and constant schedule slips.

Detection   Ask whether component testing is being done. If the answer is yes, ask for a complete description of the process.

Extraction   Institute a simple white box testing process, picking key (troublesome) objects to start with. Have the tester (who, due to lack of time, resources, and available skills, will probably be another engineer on the project) go through the source code method by method and do a code review, devising a test plan for each method as the test proceeds. This action alone will probably be enough to flush out any number of bugs. Then have the tester carry out the test plan for each method, getting help as needed from the engineer in charge of that object. This is only a small start, but it will establish the concept of component testing and it will send all the engineers scrambling to clean up their code before someone does white box testing on it. You may go through a bit of code instability because of the scrambling, but then things will start to improve.

Prevention From the project's beginning, insist on access to the resources and time necessary to do component testing. Build white box or black box testing into the schedule. Get it done.

Pitfall 9.3: Thinking about testing after the fact.

So far, we've talked about the combinatorial explosion of object-object relationships and the need to perform component testing because of the resulting complexity. You should be getting the message that testing object-oriented systems is a challenge that requires a significant investment to work well.

Unfortunately, it is often the case that testing—and thinking about testing —doesn't begin until the project reaches the alpha (feature complete) or beta (fully functional) stage. With traditional software development, there was often nothing to test until alpha was reached, although enlightened development groups performed component testing of subroutines and function libraries. Engineering groups are often suspicious of SQA testers—and they don't want to look bad—so they tend to avoid turning over a working program to testers as long as possible. Upper management, accustomed to traditional develop-first-test-later cycles, is often unwilling to pay for testing early in the development cycle—especially for engineers with the skills to do white box and black box component testing.

It is especially crucial that engineers consider testing, especially component testing, from the very start. Otherwise, the resulting architecture may be too convoluted to easily allow component testing. That same convolution will increase product instability and will hinder regular user testing as well.

Symptoms   Engineers saying things like, "Just go ahead and put that in; we'll test it for bugs later." No time (or money) allocated in the schedule for testing until the last few months before delivery.

Consequences   Significant schedule slippage as testing takes much longer than anyone (except possibly the SQA people) anticipated.

Detection   Look at the project's status and ask, "What testing or preparation for testing is going on right now? What more could we be doing?" If you're not happy with the answers, then take steps. If you are happy with the answers, go back and reread the previous two pitfalls to make sure that you're not fooling yourself.

Extraction   This is difficult in midstream except on a limited basis, unless you have an open-ended schedule. A good start is the component testing approach described in the **Extraction** section of the previous pitfall. Work with your SQA counterpart (if you have one) to figure out how to start phasing in testing as soon as possible.

Prevention   When the project begins, plan for constant, ongoing testing. This can include the following:

- Require a component white or black box test plan for every object and subsystem created.
- Treat component design reviews as a form of testing.
- Have engineers embed the appropriate trace, dump, and assert commands into their code.
- Have the project architecture support (if possible) logging all method calls, including sender, receiver, method name, parameter list, and receiver state before and after the call.
- Have engineers build **workbenches**—miniprograms that can be used to drive object and subsystem components for white box and black box testing.
- Require that new versions of components undergo white and black box testing before they are released into the general project.

This process involves a lot of testing, but it will pay off significantly in code stability and correctness, and probably in total time-to-completion.

Pitfall 9.4: Underestimating testing and support requirements and costs.

Project testing and support are often treated as an afterthought, both in terms of planning and in terms of financial budgeting. The unspoken (or sometimes spoken) idea is that you develop the project, let some testers pound on it for a week or two, fix a few bugs, release it, and forget about it.

That's a recipe for disaster—in the form of a late shipment or a buggy product—even under the best of circumstances. By contrast, in *The Mythical Man Month* Brooks estimates that testing takes one-half of the total development cycle time. As you've seen in this chapter, object-oriented development does not offer the best of circumstances because it introduces more test challenges, not fewer. Because OOD tends to reduce development time, using OOD implies that testing will take an even greater percentage of the total time. Yet upper management and many engineers think that it should be less.

The same problem appears in the jobs of supporting and maintaining the project once it is released. However, that later stage provides the opportunity to leverage the investment in object technology by seeking to generalize solutions and make the architecture more modular and reusable. Yet that is also the point when investment in the project dwindles.

Symptoms   Lack of budget, personnel, and schedule time for testing and support.

Consequences   Late projects; sometimes very late or dead projects; engineers and support personnel dragged away from other tasks to support project after release.

Detection   First test: Did you schedule one-half of your total project time for testing?

Second test: Are you dealing with managing object combinatorials, component testing, and building for testing ahead of time?

Third test: Are you having trouble getting the money, people, and time necessary to do testing and support?

If you've answered no to one or more of these questions, then you may be in trouble.

Extraction   First, use this and the other pitfalls in this chapter to reevaluate your plans for testing and support. Put together a new plan that includes factor reduction, component testing, and proactive engineer testing support.

Second, reset expectations with upper management. Good luck.

Prevention   The majority of the time spent in object-oriented development should be focused on two activities: design and testing. Actual implementation tends to be a very small part of the project cycle, especially because of the nature of OOD and the support tools available. If you focus your schedule on design-and-test, it will shift the mindset of your engineers, your testers, and (with luck) upper management.

Conclusion

Implementing the suggestions in this chapter may not be easy. It can be difficult to get resources from upper management. It can be hard to convince engineers to work directly with testers during development. It can be tough to train testers in OOD to the degree necessary to make them effective component testers.

Start with a small pilot project, one that involves only a few people and is of short duration. Use this project as a test bed and a training ground. Then repeat the process with different people. Results win converts; the more you can do this and get the necessary results, the more support you will get.

References

Brooks, Frederick P., Jr. *The Mythical Man-Month*, Reading, Mass: Addison-Wesley, 1979.

CHAPTER 10:
REUSE PITFALLS

Nothing can have value without being an object of utility. If it be useless, the labor contained in it is useless, cannot be reckoned as labor, and cannot therefore create value.

—Karl Marx, *Capital*

Software reuse—building new projects from objects and subsystems created in earlier projects—is the benefit of object-oriented development most often touted, yet it is one of the benefits least often received...or, at least, that's how it seems.

The reason is simple: Reuse takes time and effort up front, whereas object-oriented development is promoted and adopted as a means to get software done more quickly. Because of that, the initial design effort is neglected, and the result is a lot of work after the fact to massage existing software into shape for reuse.

Even while software is being developed, you can plan for reuse by keeping track of dependencies among objects and among subsystems. It's tedious, but like the design work up front, it will pay off in the end.

The worst thing you can do is finish the project and then say, "All right, how much of this code can we reuse?" At that point, you may have to rewrite from scratch all the code that you'd like to apply to your next project. With luck, you will have learned your lesson by then.

Pitfall 10.1: Underestimating the difficulty of reuse.

Object-oriented development presents a real dilemma. First it was touted for speed of development. But it turned out that for first-time projects, OOD was more difficult and took longer—unless developers could use class libraries and other tools that provide for code reuse. So the next cry was that reuse was the boon of OOD and that the payoff would be in the long run, not the short term. Guess what? Doing OOD with the explicit goal of reuse is harder and takes longer.

Why is designing for reuse so hard? Here are some reasons:

- Reusable software must be more general—which means that it is larger and more complex and handles a wider range of cases. This in turn means that it will require more time for design, implementation, testing, and rearchitecture. Even if management supports the effort (see Pitfall 10.5), any deficiencies in the generality won't show up until reuse is attempted.

- Similarities among projects are often small. If I build three editors, chances are high that I can reuse a fair amount of code—but if the editors are that similar, one wonders why I'm building three of them.On the other hand, if I build an editor, a database front-tend, and an account management application, the amount of code that is reusable will tend to decrease.

- Much of what is and can be reused among disparate applications is already provided by the application environment or operating system. These features include input/output, the user interface, memory management, and so on. This benefit is increased when you have access to object class libraries from which you can subclass.

- The universe in which projects live is in constant flux. This universe includes (but is not limited to) the following:
  - input devices (keyboard, mouse, etc.)
  - output devices (monitor, printer, etc.)
  - system configurations (CPU, memory, mass storage)
  - software environment (operating system, application environment, other applications)
  - information sources (files, file systems, networks, data feeds, databases)

- actual and targeted users and their needs, demands, and expectations.

If the real universe were in this much flux, we'd have to handcraft everything, too, throwing away or upgrading our old possessions as soon as they ceased to work effectively.

Symptoms A casual or cavalier attitude toward the challenge of reuse. Overly optimistic assumptions of how much code can and will be reused.

Consequences Either significant schedule slippage or very little reuse.

Detection Conduct a survey among developers and technical managers, asking them to identify reuse candidates in the existing and planned code base. As candidates are identified, ask the developers how each class or subsystem might be reused, and what (if any) extra work will be necessary to achieve reuse.

If everyone seems quite optimistic, pick one candidate and conduct a mini-project to actually reuse it in a small application. Note the time and effort required; you may have to pull the plug on the project before completion.

Extraction The survey process in **Detection** should help wake up everyone. Complete the survey, discuss it, and present the findings to upper management so that they have a better understanding of the difficulty of reuse.

Prevention Keep reminding yourself and everyone else about the challenges of reuse.

Throughout the analysis and design phases (you *are* doing analysis and design, aren't you?), include reuse as a consideration for every class and subsystem proposed.

Pitfall 10.2: Having or setting unrealistic expectations.

This is the biggest pitfall in the whole area of software reuse: You or your boss or your boss's boss expects that most of the software developed for a given project can be reused in subsequent projects. This is seldom the case.

There are several reasons that expectations for reuse are unrealistic. First and foremost is the hype surrounding object-oriented development. Article after article, especially in the business magazines, talks about objects being the "building blocks" of more complex software systems. All this overlooks the fact that all we can build from building blocks are toy structures that fall when bumped. Real structures, especially those being built to order (such as a custom home), may use standard components but require a lot of manual cutting, fitting, binding, and shaping.

Second, the reuse domain may be unrealistic. Standard tools and components for building a house may have a high degree of reuse when building another house, but most of the house components will be worthless when building a pool. In the same way, objects and subsystems created for one application may have very little relevance for another—yet expectations of reuse may not take that into account.

Third, expectations for reuse may outstrip the skills and experience of the developers involved. Consider the pitfalls in the rest of this chapter. Stumbling into any of them may cause reusability of the code produced to fall far short of what is expected.

Symptoms　Schedules for new projects keep getting shortened because of "all the code we can reuse" from current projects.

Consequences　Unhappy managers, including upper management; slippage on subsequent projects.

Detection　Ask questions. Ask engineers about specific classes and subsystems and how well they can be reused. Then ask managers what degree of reuse they expect and plan on. Then ask upper management what they expect to be the development time of subsequent projects.

If everyone seems happy, a second check is to take one of the subsystems or some of classes that your developers expect to reuse and have an engineer attempt to create a new and separate project that uses them. This will give a quick indication of whether these components can be readily reused.

Extraction   First, assign an engineer to evaluate—much as described in **Detection**—all of the subsystems and classes in the current project that the developers expect to reuse. This process will give you a better idea of the actual likelihood of reuse.

Second, use the information from this exercise to reset expectations up and down the chain: engineers, technical managers, upper management. Make sure that everyone understands why reuse may not be as high as anticipated. Third, if reuse is critical and resources are available, prioritize the components and assign one or more developers to clean them up for reuse. If possible, merge them back into the current project, although that may be too high a risk.

Prevention   During project design and architecture, take time to clearly identify the components that are likely candidates for reuse and those that are not. Make sure that everyone understands the differences and the reasons for classifying them in each category.

Pitfall 10.3: Being too focused on code reuse

This may sound like a strange pitfall, given all that has been said about the reuse benefits of object-oriented development. But that's exactly the problem: Reuse as a metric is too often interpreted to mean "the number of lines of previously written code that were used in the new project." That can lead to several problems.

Code reuse is seen as the end, not the means. Be aware of this: There is nothing inherently good about reuse. It is of benefit only to the degree that it enables you to create new, derived, or modified applications more quickly, less expensively, and with higher quality. Focusing on a "lines of code reused" metric can be as meaningless and self-defeating as the classic "lines of code" metric.

Design reuse is often neglected in favor of code reuse. The most important creation to come from an OOD project is often the architecture and design, not the code implementation. This is true for two reasons: First, the implementation may be too specific to the application (see Pitfall 10.1), whereas the design and architecture may be more general. Second, the implementation may be tied to a given language or environment, whereas the design and architecture can be more readily ported elsewhere.

Too little abstraction is done at the application framework level. Pitfalls 10.1 and 10.2 noted that an application seldom contains a great deal of code that can be directly reused in another. However, just about every application can be built from a common framework, which makes the framework one of the prime candidates for reuse. Unfortunately, a focus on code reuse tends to ignore application frameworks in favor of more specific and "tangible" classes and subsystems.

In short, too great a focus on "lines of code reused" may blind or block you from the real payoff possibilities.

Symptoms   Dictated or implied expectations of significant code reuse, particularly from upper management.

Consequences Unnecessary delays. Slipped schedules. Reuse benefits fail to meet expectations.

Detection   Survey all relevant parties about their expectations of code reuse. Test their reaction to suggestions that design and framework reuse is more important and that code reuse is relatively unimportant.

Extraction   Look for opportunities for design and framework reuse in current development efforts. Educate all relevant parties about those possibilities.

Prevention   Set expectations in advance that reuse will be primarily in design and application framework, and develop with that in mind. Ironically, by doing so you will probably end up with significant code reuse as well.

Pitfall 10.4: Not investing in reuse.

So far, we've looked at the problems of not understanding how hard it is to code for reuse, of having too high expectations, and of being too focused on code reuse. These are all major issues, but the most common pitfall is this: expecting reuse to come for free.

Reuse is difficult, which means that reuse costs. It costs time. It costs money. It costs effort in analysis, design, implementation, and testing. It may cost additional staff. And that's not what upper management wants to hear. Far more likely is the scenario painted by Henderson-Sellers and Pant: "In current practice, end-lifecycle positioning simply leads to the completion of the first product, the start of the second, and a total omission of the generalization activity on the grounds of there being no 'time'."

And given all the costs, risks, and pitfalls associated with your first object-oriented development project, the last thing that upper management wants is to spend more money and drag out the process.

Symptoms   Lack of resources for reuse. Lack of support for investing resources in reuse.

Consequences   Lack of reuse.

Detection   Evaluate how much development for reuse is occurring. Float a trial balloon to invest more resources, and consider the response.

Extraction   Set or reset expectations of costs and benefits. If you still have a job, see **Prevention** below for possible models for reuse. Pick the most likely acceptable plan to upper management and pitch it.

Prevention   OOD in general and reuse in particular must be pitched as a long-term investment. You need to do that as early as possible.

Henderson-Sellers and Pant identify four reuse models for software development. They are:

- End-lifecycle model: Do the generalization after delivering a project. Unfortunately, that may be the hardest time to get resources; see the scenario above.
- G-C1 model: Do the generalization before delivering a project "so that the customer pays for it."
- Two-library model: Set aside potentially reusable components; generalize them as time permits and then move them into a library of generalized components.

- Alternative core-technology model: Establish a core technology group (perhaps only one person) whose only job is to generalize components developed for ongoing projects.

Each model has its own investment considerations and can be adjusted to meet your needs. However, you will end up using one or more of these models in order to achieve reuse, so plan accordingly.

Pitfall 10.5: Generalizing after the fact.

Two major problems occur while objects with potential for reuse are being developed. The first is that the object or subsystem starts out with a good, general design and slowly becomes more and more specific to the project at hand. The reason is well known to any engineer: It is usually easier and faster to write a specific solution than a general one. And because of time pressure to fix bugs and complete functionality, time and again engineers face pressure—from themselves, from their manager, from the upper echelons of the company, from the customers—to just make the thing work and not worry about an "elegant" solution. Of course, the story changes after the project is complete; then everyone wants to know where all the benefits of object-oriented development are, although they were unwilling to pay the price for those benefits up front.

The second problem is at least as common. The object or subsystem is not designed or implemented with reuse in mind, but an effort to ensure reuse occurs late in the development cycle or after the project is completed. At that point, it is often both unsafe and difficult to rewrite the object or subsystem to be able to reuse it in other projects because of the implicit and explicit dependencies that have crept in.

Symptoms   Lack of code reuse; engineers complaining about not being given time to do things right or having to resort to "quick and dirty" implementations.

Consequences Lack of code reuse.

Detection   Review the class hierarchy with the engineering team and ask them to evaluate the reuse possibilities for each class. Review each class and check it both for general utility and for project dependencies.

Extraction   Identify a class or subsystem that is likely to be useful in subsequent projects. Analyze its specific behavior and see whether it can be minimized or whether the general behavior can be pushed into a superclass. Have an engineer do the generalization and try to integrate the new version back into the current project.

It can be hard to do this for a project under way, especially if the schedule is already at risk (and when is it not at risk?). There's a real chance of schedule slip, both because of the engineer assignment and the risk when the generalized class or subsystem is integrated back into the project.

Prevention   Component reuse must be planned for and designed from the start. This means anticipating the various ways you might use a given component and building it accordingly. You can first apply the techniques described in **Extraction.** A better solution may be to identify subsequent projects so that the developers can design components with future use in mind. The best solution is probably to have multiple projects under way simultaneously so that the code must be used in and usable by all the projects.

Pitfall 10.6: Allowing too many connections.

The biggest hindrance to code reuse comes from dependencies and connections. Let's review the example that was presented in the Primer. Suppose we have a WeatherClock class that is a subclass of TimePiece. It also contains instances of Thermometer, Barometer, and HumidityGauge, all of which are subclasses of WeatherGauge, which in turn refers to the Atmosphere object class.

Without even trying, we've identified six additional classes that must come along if we try to reuse WeatherClock in another program. We have yet to see what additional dependencies there might be in any of these seven classes. And this was a fairly clean, simple design. A complex object class may have a dozen or more other object classes to which it refers, each of which will have its own list of dependencies, and so on.

It's important to remember that most code reuse doesn't come from classes yanked out of one project and stuck into another. It comes from base classes that can be reused or subclassed in other projects. This means that dependencies on base classes are usually less critical than dependencies on derived classes—although in languages with lots of lightweight root classes (such as C++), that may not be the case.

Symptoms Long lists of referenced classes in the interface or implementation of a given class.

Consequences Lack of code reuse.

Detection Pick a useful class to be reused for a subsequent project. Try to bring it over to that project. See how many classes must come with it, and how many classes must come with each of those classes, and so on.

Extraction Identify a class or subsystem likely to be useful in subsequent projects. Analyze all the dependencies and see whether they can be reduced. Analyze each of the classes for which dependencies still exist. Keep working until you identify a chunk that can be safely extracted. Have an engineer do the generalization and then try to integrate the new version back into the current project.

This is a high-risk process and may not be worth the effort unless the current project is not very far along.

Prevention Again, you have to plan for component reuse and design it into the project from the start. Class dependencies should be mapped out during the analysis and design phases and should be tracked as implementation proceeds. By identifying early in the process the classes that are targeted for reuse, your developers will be better able to focus their design and implementation efforts.

Pitfall 10.7: Allowing circular dependencies.

It is possible (and not uncommon) in complex object-oriented systems for circular dependencies to occur. A circular dependency is one in which you start with a given class, A, and trace its functional and relational dependencies until you get back to class A.

Note that a circular dependency is not the same as tight cohesion within a framework or subsystem. Within a framework or subsystem, you may have several classes that talk with and depend on each other. That is not unusual and may even be necessary in order to build a subsystem or framework that can stand on its own.

The problem with circular dependencies occurs when they loop through two or more subsystems. Here's a functional case: Suppose that you have a subsystem that is responsible for laying out a set of objects on a grid according to a certain pattern. When one object of a particular kind is placed on the grid, the values it holds trigger a different subsystem that causes the object to rearrange some components inside it (and therefore modify the "shape" of the object). The reshaped object tries to fit into its current location on the grid, so it calls the grid layout subsystem again, and so on.

Here's a contrived, although possible, referential example. Suppose you have three subsystems: one for graphical rendering, a second one for text rendering, and a third one for line layout. The text rendering subsystem uses some graphical rendering calls, the line layout system uses some text rendering calls, and the graphical rendering subsystem uses some line layout calls. It then becomes impossible to reuse any one of the three subsystems without bringing along the other two (and anything else they might require).

Symptoms   Inability to extract and reuse code cleanly because of circular dependencies.

Consequences   Lack of code reuse.

Detection   There's no easy way. You can identify a class that you want to extract or reuse and start tracing all its dependencies. If you get back to that class, then you need to see where and how to break the chain.

Extraction   Again, this is a high-risk process, and one that may not be worth the effort unless the current project is not very far along.

Prevention   Once more, with feeling: *Component reuse must be planned for and designed into a project from the start*. Class dependencies should be mapped out during the analysis and design phases and should be tracked as implementation proceeds. Identifying early in the process which classes are targeted for reuse will help focus design and implementation efforts.

Conclusion

I probably sound like a broken record, but here are the principles of successful software reuse for object-oriented development:

- Reuse is most commonly achieved via class hierarchies—pushing general behavior into base classes and using those classes or subclassing them as needed in your new projects. There is a growing trend toward reuse via domain frameworks, which are collections of object classes that work together to achieve a particular end.
- Spend the time and resources necessary to track dependencies and interactions, particularly among objects or subsystems that you hope to reuse.
- Plan and design for reuse before a single line of code is written.
- Promote reuse by running two or more projects simultaneously, forcing developers to create classes and subsystems that can be shared by all projects.

And in all this, recognize that efforts to create reusable software are subject to the same rules as the rest of OOD, which means that you'll probably rearchitect two or three times before you begin in order to get it right. Plan for that.

References

Henderson-Sellers, B. and Y.R. Pant, "Adopting the reuse mindset throughout the life-cycle." *Object Magazine* 3(4), Nov/Dec 1993.

PART III

MAKING IT WORK

Place in the hands of the King of Prussia the strongest possible military power, then he will be able to carry out the policy you wish; this policy cannot succeed through speeches, and shooting-matches, and songs; it can only be carried out through blood and iron.

— Prince Bismarck (1862)

And so we come to the end of the pitfalls—at least, the ones that made it into this book. You've spent lots and lots of pages reading what not to do; it's time to be a bit more proactive.

Every pitfall had a section entitled **Extraction**. This contained hints and recommendations for what to do when you found yourself in the middle of an OOD project when falling into a given pitfall. Well, the first section of this chapter gives the same kind of advice, but on a more general level: Suggestions for what to do you do if you're in the middle of a significant OOD project and you run into serious problems. A ten-step program is offered to help you extract yourself and get the project back on track.

Every pitfall also had a section entitled **Prevention**, which talked about how to avoid the pitfall in the first place. The second section of this chapter summarizes those principles, which are intended to help you to actively plan in advance to make your OOD project a success.

The chapter—and the book—ends with final comments of my own.

Making a Mid-Course Correction

OK, so you're in the middle of an object-oriented development project, and things aren't going so well. You've been going through this book, and you recognize many of the pitfalls from experience. You want to get things back on track. What do you do?

Here's a ten-point program to do just that. Some of these steps may be difficult; others may be impossible, more for political reasons than for technical ones. But that determination in and of itself tells you whether the project is feasible. So, let's start.

1. **Suspend all development.** George Santayana once said that fanaticism consists of redoubling your efforts when you have forgotten your aim. Too many software projects are run that way, with predictable results. There's a good chance you may dig a deeper hole if you keep pushing ahead, so stop until you know exactly where

233

you're going. Have developers spend any free time studying object-oriented development and teaching one another about it.

2. **Throw out the current schedule.** Chances are it's inaccurate and doesn't allocate enough time. Such as schedule has two bad side effects: It raises false expectations for upper management, and it demoralizes the development team.

3. **Do a design, feature, and code review.** Review the project architecture, class hierarchies, and classes. Use the pitfalls in this book as a guideline to look for problems areas and deficiencies. Make a list of all current and potential problems, as well as tasks to be done.

   For each feature, find out exactly what is working and list everything that must be done to complete it, especially noting any fundamental architectural and subsystem work Then list everything that needs to be done that somehow isn't covered by a given feature.

   Review each class implementation, as well as any other non-class code that might be involved.

4. **Evaluate the project feasibility.** At this point, you should have a good idea of the state of the project, and a rough idea of the amount of work it will take to complete the project, including additional design work (if necessary), implementation, and testing. You should also know upper management's expectations and requirements. This will lead you to one of four conclusions, most likely the second or the third:

   • The project is on or ahead of schedule, and you have time to make corrections;

   • The project is behind schedule, but tolerably so;

   • The project has significant problems and cannot meet the current schedule with anything close to the current specifications;

   • The project is dead; that is, not feasible given progress to date and limitations on schedule and budget.

   If the project is on time or ahead of schedule, use the time to make corrections. If the project is dead, pull the plug and either start over or abandon it. In the other two cases—the project is behind schedule, but can be finished—then proceed with the next step.

5. **Renegotiate features, specification, and schedule.** Meet with upper management, customers, and anyone else involved. Explain that the project can be completed, but only by extending the schedule or reducing functionality. If they agree to proceed, then work with them on these three steps:

- *Perform feature triage.* Assign each feature in the specification to one of three groups: Features that absolutely must be in this release of the project; those that are negotiable; and those that can wait for a subsequent release. Throw out the features in the last group (updating the specification appropriately) and list the negotiable features in order of priority.

- *Revise the specification.* Go through the specification and update it to drop out as much as possible. Make sure everyone signs off on it.

- *Renegotiate the schedule.* Do not commit to a delivery date. Instead, insist each of the relevant parties determine the latest possible date for delivery.

6. **Evaluate every feature.** For each feature that remains (must-have and negotiable), find out exactly what works now and list every feature that still needs work to complete it, especially if any fundamental architectural or subsystem work is involved. For every feature being dropped, find out how much work is involved to clearly "tie it off." Then list everything that must be done that isn't covered by a given feature.

7. **Prioritize and estimate all tasks.** List every task generated by the previous item, order them according to relative priority and interdependencies, and estimate the time for (re)design, implementation, testing, and review for each one.

8. **Build a development schedule.** This needs to be done to accommodate your background, your development team, the task at hand, and other relevant factors. Consider using a multicycle development approach, with each cycle having design, implementation, testing, and review phases. Be sure to leave time in for continuing education on OOD. Work on this until you either run out of tasks or run out of schedule.

9. **Present the schedule.** If your schedule has you going past the "latest possible date" without accomplishing all required tasks, then go back to Step 5 and get more time or throw out more features.

10. **Implement the development plan.** Proceed, keeping a careful eye on how things are going. If you use a multicycle approach, do a reevaluation at the end of each cycle and repeat any of the above steps as required.

This is not the ideal way to run a software development project. This is intended as field surgery to help you get the project done and out the door, while laying the groundwork to make corrections later. Once you have finished that, look to the next section for some hints and tips for how to do things better the next time around.

Starting a New OOD Project

Now suppose you're new to object-oriented development, or at least not as experienced as you'd like. Or maybe the last project just didn't go as well as you wish. You now need to plan and start a new OOD project, and you want it to come in on schedule and under budget.

Here's a list of steps to help you achieve that—so long as you understand that you may have to revise both the budget and the schedule before you get started.

- **Educate yourself before you start.** Go through the bibliography and read as many of the books under "General Software Engineering" as you can; absolutely read *The Mythical Man-Month*. Do selected but significant reading from books listed under "Object-Oriented Development." Subscribe to some of the listed magazines and journals. Attend relevant seminars and trade shows. Jot down in a notebook all the ideas you have and key concepts that you need to remember.

- **Build your team wisely.** Pick developers known for self-discipline, meeting deadlines, and good team skills. If you can get some or all members with solid OOD skills, then do so—but only if they meet the other criteria. Let them know there will be a chief architect and make sure they buy into that structure completely.

- **Educate your team.** Strengthen their OOD background the same way you strengthened yours. Create a cult of learning, with an emphasis on sharing information gleaned from various sources.

- **Establish and enforce development standards.** These range from symbol naming conventions and code formatting to object-oriented metrics, and include rules and principles of OOD. For good examples of the latter, look at *Effective C++* and *Taligent's Guide to Designing Programs* (both listed in the Bibliography). Produce a written guide and have everyone sign off on the document, and make it clear they are expected to adhere to it.

- **Learn about object-oriented analysis and design methodologies.** Many books give explicit steps to follow (see the Bibliography). Study these and devise an explicit process to use in your own OOD. Do not begin analysis and design (much less implementation!) until a methodology is in place to guide you through all the steps to completion.

- **Implement a multicycle development approach.** Treat development as a series of cycles. Each cycle typically contains the following steps, although in varying proportions:

- Analysis and design

- Prototyping (user interface, class interface, hierarchy)

- Implementation

- Testing

- Review and risk assessment

Keep cycles short so that the development team can experience closure on a regular basis, but not so short that time and focus are lost while thrashing around. Plan two explicit rearchitecture cycles, to take place between regular development cycles.

- **Evaluate and select the appropriate environment and tools.** The major decision—target environment—may be out of your hands, but you will likely have a choice of language and supporting tools. Be prepared to over-invest, to try out several tools in order to find the right ones.

- **Experiment with one or two small projects.** Before starting on the large project, try a few small ones. Use the small project as an opportunity to play around with and establish team roles. Make the process fun, intense, and short, and provide some kind of team payoff at the end. Do a group review at the end of each project and make appropriate changes.

- **Get involved with the customers.** Before you even start analysis and design, find out who are the customers and spend time with them. Find out what they really want and need. Use prototypes and white boards to sketch out different approaches. Observe customers working with different user interfaces; find out what's natural and what's hard to understand.

- **Appoint a chief architect.** Win team buy-in by clearly emphasizing their opportunities to contribute and the fact that implementation is more intellectually challenging.

- **Plan testing in advance and involve testers from the start.** Work with SQA to develop test plans and standards so that testing can be conducted each cycle, not just when development is finished.

- **If you want reuse, design for it from the start.** If possible, find out what will be the subsequent projects. Do simple design work on each and identify areas for possible reuse.

- **Start out stupid, and work up from there.** Keep the scope of each development cycle manageable, so that if you run into problems all of your tasks and risks are more manageable.

- **Underpromise and overdeliver.** Show prototypes to customers only in order to get feedback and direction; make sure their lack of functionality is clear. Be conservative about scheduling and aggressive about development. Underplay advances; leave yourself as much slack in the schedule as possible.

- **Nail down a detailed specification and stick to it.** Make sure that both the customer representative and upper management sign off on the specification. Make it as explicit as possible, including a prioritized feature list. If customers or upper management come back to you with requests for new features, make it clear that the schedule and the development plan must be renegotiated to accommodate them.

- **Get tangible results early.** This lets you gauge your progress and get feedback from your customers. By doing so, you can earn the right to stop development and reschedule if necessary.

- **Re-evaluate the specification and schedule on a regular basis.** Make sure you're still on track; alert upper management and make adjustments if you're not.

As noted above, there are many excellent books that can do a better and more thorough job of telling you what to do and how to do it. Get them, read them, learn from them, and apply what they tell you.

Afterword

It was Benjamin Franklin, in *Poor Richard's Almanac,* who said "Experience keeps a dear [expensive] school, but fools will learn in no other." More fools we, then, who for twenty-five years have had the time, opportunity, and experience to learn how best to conduct software development in general, and object-oriented development in particular, yet persist in making the same errors time and again.

But the stakes have risen in twenty-five years. Back in 1970, national and global economies, businesses, militaries, and governments were not as heavily dependent on software as they are today. That dependence grows daily and with it the need for increasingly complex and more reliable software, which must be delivered in a timely fashion. Our struggles to deliver that software have an impact beyond what we might have otherwise assumed.

Pointing fingers has little merit; there is more than enough blame to spread among upper management, technical managers, developers, and anyone else who might influence the process. But I will note Adele Goldberg's comment from 1992 that "Fear [of the competition] and greed are selling [OOD] tools." She has since noted that logic and reason now have their roles in that decision. But so long as fear and greed drive the software development process, the resulting software will suffer. To those who would argue that fear and greed are healthy signs of capitalism, I simply respond: That's fine, but do you want those to be the guiding factors behind the design and development of the cars you drive, the planes you fly in, or the medications you take? I for one hope that the firms creating those products take quality, integrity, and reliability very seriously. But it's hard to expect that kind of dedication from others, if we who develop software are unwilling to live up to those same standards.

Enough of the heavy stuff. Here's hoping that somehow we can find the time, resources, and environment to build truly great software, and that this book helps us all to dodge a few bullets and avoid a few pitfalls.

References

Goldberg, Adele. "Wishful thinking," *Object Magazine* 2(3), Sep/Oct 1992.

Meyers, Scott. *Effective* C++. Reading, Mass.: Addison-Wesley, 1992.

Taligent, Inc. *Taligent's Guide to Designing Programs*. Reading, Mass.: Addison-Wesley, 1994.

BIBLIOGRAPHY AND RESOURCES

Progress, far from consisting in change, depends on retentiveness...Those who cannot remember the past are condemned to fulfill it.

—George Santayana, *Life of Reason*

One theme throughout this book is the need to educate everyone involved in object-oriented development and do so in a way appropriate to their responsibilities. That's what this section is all about.

The possible sources of information are constantly changing, so this section makes no effort at all at completeness. Indeed, an exhaustive list would leave you with too many choices and little direction. Instead, I've put together a list of books that would be mandatory reading or reference were I starting an object-oriented development group from scratch. These books are grouped into three categories:

- Those dealing with general software engineering;
- Those dealing directly with object-oriented development;
- Those dealing with specific environments and languages.

I own copies of most these books, and I've studied all of them to some extent, so I can vouch for them. Your mileage may vary, so look them over before buying them. The final part of this section deals with other resources available to you: magazines, journals, and so on.

This list is a bit of a hodge-podge, but represents a first pass of suggestions that you read these if you read nothing else. A lot of what has been learned about software engineering during the past thirty years has been in vain, because no one takes the time to read about it. The idea here is to help you avoid errors that many have made before; it's interesting (and perhaps significant) that the oldest books are in many ways the most relevant and timeless.

Books: General Software Engineering

The Mythical Man-Month

Frederick P. Brooks, Addison-Wesley, Reading, Mass., 1979.

The *sine qua non* of software engineering and project management. Every person involved in object-oriented development, from the CEO to the most junior engineer, should read this book and believe what it says, because it's true, whether you want it to be or not.

Peopleware

Tom De Marco and Timothy Lister, Dorset House Publishing Co., New York, 1987.

An excellent book on the details of setting up and running an effective software development department. As with *The Mythical Man-Month*, you ignore this book at your own peril.

Software State-of-the-Art

Tom De Marco and Timothy Lister, editors. Dorset House Publishing, New York, 1990.

An excellent, if occasionally uneven, selection of 31 papers on software engineering the 1980s; this makes a good follow-on to Ed Yourdon's two collections (see below). Contains Fred Brooks' classic, "No Silver Bullet", but there's something to learn from every paper...except, maybe, the one on ray tracing Jell-O.

Software Engineering Productivity Handbook

Jessica Keyes (editor), Windcrest/McGraw-Hill, New York, 1993.

If Brooks' thin volume establishes the framework, this thick one (37 contributors, 69 short chapters) fills in many details. The first chapter alone, Keyes' survey of the field, would make the book worthwhile for most development groups but it contains so much more.

Debugging the Development Process

Steve Maguire, Microsoft Press, Redmond, Wash., 1994.

An honest and useful book about trying to get products out the door, from someone who should know. You might also want to check out another of his books, *Writing Solid Code*.

Software Engineering: A Practitioner's Approach (2nd ed.)

Roger S. Pressman, McGraw-Hill Book Co., New York, 1987.

An excellent one-volume survey of the concepts, issues, and practices of software engineering, including one of the earlier chapters published on object-oriented design. A good book to review on a regular basis to avoid reinventing the wheel (especially if it's a square one).

Productivity Sand Traps and Tar Pits

Mike Walsh, Dorset House Publishing, New York, 1991.

I bought this book thinking it would be another tome dealing with software engineering. Instead, it is a very candid look at management and politics within corporate MIS departments, with an emphasis on how to survive in that environment.

The Art of 'Ware

Bruce F. Webster, M&T Books, New York, in press.

Based on Sun Tzu's *The Art of War*, this book discusses issues governing technology development, management, and product marketing, especially within a start-up company. I'm not sure it belongs in the company of these other books, but it does apply Sun Tzu's brilliance to modern development challenges.

The Psychology of Computer Programming

Gerald M. Weinberg, Van Nostrand Reinhold Company, New York, 1971.

I'm not sure this book is still in print, but every time I reread my copy (bought in 1978) I'm amazed at how true Weinberg's observations remain. Most books by Weinberg are worth reading.

Classics in Software Engineering

Edward Yourdon (editor), Yourdon Press, New York, 1979.

This is the single best collection of the classic papers (24 in all) that launched the discipline of software engineering. Even the authors are classics: Djikstra, Boehm, Baker, Wirth, McCracken, Kernighan, Plauger, Knuth, DeMarco. You might also want to look at the follow-up volume, *Writings of the Revolution* (1982).

Decline & Fall of the American Programmer

Edward Yourdon, Yourdon Press, Englewood Cliffs, NJ, 1992.

A provocative work on why American programmers are (or appear to be) fat, lazy, overpaid and underproductive. Well-worth reading; don't miss the appendix on The Programmer's Bookshelf, which lists the books you should study when you finish this one.

Books: Object-Oriented Development

A flood of books on object-oriented development has hit the market, so this list will be incomplete, small, and selective—perhaps scandalously so—especially given the large number of titles now out or due for publication soon. Note that many chapters in this book have additional titles listed at the end.

Object Oriented Design with Applications (2nd ed.)

Grady Booch, Benjamin/Cummings Publishing Co. Inc., Redwood City, Calif., 1994.

It says much about the nature of object-oriented development or, perhaps, of Booch's standards of excellence, that this second edition was published just three years after the first edition. It is possibly the best single-volume introduction to OOD, but it can be a bit intimidating for some engineers and overwhelming for the non-technical. Explains the (revised) Booch notation for OOD.

Object Development Methods

Andy Carmichael, (editor). SIGS Books, New York, 1994.

An excellent single-volume survey of object-oriented development methodologies, as well as discussion of issues surrounding OOD.

Object-Oriented Analysis (2nd ed.)

Object-Oriented Design

Peter Coad and Edward Yourdon, Yourdon Press, Englewood Cliffs, NJ, 1991.

These two books are proof that the concepts of object-oriented development don't have to be complex or hard to understand. The first book focuses on domain analysis; the second, on creating design components (human interaction, problem domain, task management, data management). Don't be fooled by how thin the two volumes are; they contain more than enough information inside to keep you busy. See also Coad's book with Jill Nicola, *Object-Oriented Programming* (Yourdon Press, 1993).

Object-Oriented Development: The Fusion Method

Derek Coleman, *et alis*. Prentice-Hall, Englewood Cliffs, NJ, 1994.

Presents the Fusion OOD methodology, which incorporates aspects of OMT (Rumbaugh et alis), Booch, CRC, and formal software engineering methods.

Succeeding with Objects: Decision Frameworks for Project Management

Goldberg, Adele and Kenneth Rubin, Addison-Wesley, Reading, MA, 1995.

Rather than giving a one-size-fits-all approach to OOD, Goldberg and Rubin go up one level and tell you how to create a process that will work for your particular needs and constraints. A good counterpoint to this book: mine tells you how you might fail, while theirs tells you how you might succeed.

Design Patterns: Elements of Reusable Object-Oriented Software

Erich Gamma, Richard Helm, Ralph Johnson, and John Vlissides; Addison-Wesley, Reading, Mass., 1995.

This is a must-have. The book presents a set of 23 patterns in object design and implementation grouped into three categories: creation, structure, and behavior. Buy this book and study it before you get started on design.

Object-Oriented Software Metrics

Mark Lorenz and Jeff Kidd, Prentice-Hall, Englewood Cliffs, NJ, 1994.

The first published (in book form) collection of metrics for OOD, with analysis of the metrics over several projects. Its helpful, but leaves you wanting more; I hope Lorenz and Kidd do a second edition, pulling in some of the other OOD metrics found in the literature and do a more extensive survey of applying them.

Object Lessons

Tom Love, SIGS Books, New York, 1993.

Love's book takes a step back from doing object-oriented development to look at the issues surrounding it. An excellent book for upper management and technical managers, and one that should be read before embarking on serious OOD.

Object-Oriented Modeling and Design

James Rumbaugh, Michael Blaha, William Premerlani, Frederick Eddy, and William Lorensen, Prentice Hall, Englewood Cliffs, NJ, 1991.

Covers in a single volume what Coad/Yourdon/Nicola cover in three: modeling, design, and implementation. Written as a college textbook and not for the faint-of-heart, but worth having and reading. Introduces the Rumbaugh *et alis* OOD notation.

Object Lifecycles: Modeling the World in States

Sally Shlaer and Stephen J. Mellor, Yourdon Press, Englewood Cliffs, NJ, 1992.

Presents the Shlaer/Mellor methodology for object-oriented analysis (OOA). The three major components of their OOA are information modeling, state modeling, and process modeling. Builds on their earlier work, *Object-Oriented Systems Analysis*.

Object Engineering: Designing Large Scale Object-Oriented Systems

Gary C. Sullo, John Wiley & Sons, NY, 1994.

This book has a mainframe feel and I'm a workstation kind of guy, but I came away impressed with the author's methodical, logical, and complete approach to object engineering, particularly for those familiar with process- and data-oriented design.

Object-Oriented Technology: A Manager's Guide

David A. Taylor, Addison-Wesley, Reading, Mass, 1990.

Probably the best non-technical introduction to object technology concepts and issues I've seen.

Designing Object-Oriented Software

Rebecca Wirfs-Brock, Brian Wilkerson, and Lauren Wiener, Prentice-Hall, Englewood Cliffs, NJ, 1990.

Presents an OOD methodology that makes extended use of the card-based CRC (class/responsibilities/collaborators) approach.

Books: Environments and Languages

It seems as though in the computer language section of any decent public bookstore one language always takes up most of the space. First it was BASIC, then Pascal, then C, and now it's C++. But there are still literally hundreds of titles at any given time.

Because of that, this section will only point to books that I know will be of help because of experience—I own and have used them. Recommendations are welcome for future editions. I have not included here developers' reference manuals published by the manufacturers for specific environments, such as those for the Microsoft Win32 API (five volumes), NEXTSTEP (six volumes), Taligent (six volumes), and so on.

Inside OLE 2.0

Kraig Brockschmidt, Microsoft Press, Redmond, Wash., 1994.

A massive (1,000 pages) tutorial on programming for Microsoft's OLE 2.0 specification. It is undoubtedly the best book on the subject, since Brockschmidt is Microsoft's designated representative on OLE 2.0, writing articles and speaking at conferences.

Advanced C++: Programming Styles and Idioms

James O. Coplien, Addison-Wesley, Reading, Mass., 1992.

This books lies somewhere between *The Annotated C++ Reference Manual and Effective* C++ in intent and penetrability. Building on the readers knowledge of C++, this book explores what you can do with C++ and how to do it. It is not light reading, but it is worthwhile for those interested in becoming proficient at using C++.

The Annotated C++ Reference Manual

Margaret A. Ellis and Bjarne Stroustrup, Addison-Wesley, Reading, Mass., 1990.

This is just what it sounds like: the official AT&T C++ reference manual, with notes and comments by Ellis and Stroustrup. Its not light reading, but necessary to understand what the language is supposed to do.

NEXTSTEP Programming: STEP ONE: Object-Oriented Applications

Simson L. Garfinkel and Michael K. Mahoney, Springer-Verlag, NY, 1993.

This is a single-volume tutorial on NEXTSTEP programming and the best of the books out on the subject. As a bonus, it teaches Objective-C as you go along. A second book (STEP TWO) is rumored, but the first book will need to be updated for NEXTSTEP 4.0, which will use the somewhat different OpenStep API.

Discovering Smalltalk

Wilf LaLonde, Benjamin/Cummings, Redwood City, Calif., 1994.

An introduction to Smalltalk and a good lead-in to some of the weightier Smalltalk volumes.

Eiffel: The Language

Bertrand Meyer, Prentice-Hall, NY, 1992.

An introduction to the Eiffel programming language, written by its creator. This is actually one in a four-volume series by Meyer that focuses on object development using Eiffel.

Effective C++

Scott Meyers, Addison-Wesley, Reading, Mass., 1992.

If you are doing C++ programming, you absolutely must study this book. Meyers subtitled it *50 specific ways to improve your programs and designs;* he could have as easily named it. *Pitfalls of C++ Development*, but he's obviously a more upbeat guy than I am. Meyers does an outstanding job of explaining how to get the most out of C++ without getting into trouble. His book made me appreciate and even enjoy C++, which was no mean feat.

Teach Yourself...C++ (4rd ed.)

Al Stevens, MIS Press, NY, 1995.

There are dozens of books on learning C++. This one is clear, simple, logical, and painless in its approach; frankly, it's one of the best. It says that it assumes familiarity with C, but the examples start so simple that I suspect anyone with a decent programming background could use it.

The Design and Evolution of C++

Bjarne Stroustrup, Addison-Wesley, Reading, Mass., 1994.

This is a good book to have when you reach a point in your C++ studies that you want to throw things through windows. In the first place, it allows Stroustrup to explain the thinking and debates that provide insight into various aspects of C++. In the second place, it's softcover, which means it will bounce off the window when you throw it.

Taligent's Guide to Designing Programs

Taligent, Inc. Addison-Wesley, Reading, Mass., 1994.

Subtitled *Well-mannered object-oriented design in* C++, this book is worth reading even if you're not doing Taligent development. It contains guidelines for object-oriented design and C++ programming that are worth studying.

Other Resources

Some publications focus specifically on object-oriented development. Nearly all of them are published by SIGS Publications (71 West 23rd Street, 3rd Floor, New York, NY 10010). They include *C++ Report, Journal of Object-Oriented Programming, Object Magazine, Report on Object Analysis and Design*, and *The Smalltalk Report*.

The technical publications and conference proceedings of the Association for Computing Machinery (ACM) and the Institute of Electrical and Electronic Engineers (IEEE) are a rich source of articles discussing object technology and theory. These include *Communications of the ACM, IEEE Software*, and *IEEE Transactions on Software Engineering*. ACM also sponsors the annual international OOPSLA conference.

Many more magazines providing industry coverage or focusing on software development offer information about object-oriented development and its related issues. Such publications include *ComputerWorld, Computer Reseller News, InfoWorld, Open Systems Today, PC Week, BYTE, Dr. Dobb's Journal, Software Development, PC Techniques, Microsoft Systems Journal*, and others.

Electronic resources include Internet news groups focused on object development (comp.object) or specific languages (comp.lang.smalltalk, comp.lang.c++, etc.).

Of special value is the rather massive comp.object FAQ (frequently-asked questions) file, edited and maintained by Bob Hathaway of Geodesic Systems. This FAQ is posted to comp.object on a regular basis and also be accessed (as of December 1994) in the following ways:

- FTP: anonymous@zaphod.uchicago.edu:/pub/CompObj7.faq(.Z)

- Web: http://iamwww.unibe.ch/~scg/OOinfo/FAQ/index.html

- E-Mail: send mail to: mail-server@rtfm.mit.edu

    leave the Subject: field blank

    message: send usenet/comp.object/*

Finally, several trade shows are dedicated to object-development. Among them are ObjectWorld (IDG World Expo) and Object Expo (SIGS Conferences).

INDEX

A

abstract class 25

abstraction 11, 24, 118

Adams, Jayson 1

adopting objects 197

Affinito, Tom 62

Alfonso the Wise 147

analysis 26, 38, 46, 78, 103, 106, 148

application environment (see environment)

application programming interface (API) 8

architect 26, 62, 114, 117, 121, 237

architecture 22, 62, 114, 160

articles about OOD 32

assembler 9

assignment 192

association 20, 24

audience 4

B

backlash 74

base class (see also superclass) 14, 25, 170, 172, 174

basic concepts 7

benefits of OOD 21

beta testing 127

bibliography 241

binding (see message binding)

Bismarck, Prince 233

bitwise copy 192

black-box testing 206

bloated objects 180, 182

Boehm, Barry W. 82, 83

Book of Mormon, the 29

Boole, George 191

Brooks, Frederick P. 1, 37, 77, 84, 115, 210

buzzwords 1, 40

C

C++ 38, 42, 46, 114, 138, 140, 170

Cairo 131

Carter, Jimmy 72

chief architect (see architect)

circular dependencies 228

class 12, 24, 167

class hierarchy 12, 46, 116, 158, 182, 230

class method (see method)

client/server applications 23, 44

CLOS 9, 46, 131

code reuse (see also reuse) 220

coding 191

    coding standards (see standards)

    coding too soon 148

Common Development Environment (CDE) 8

Common Point (see Taligent, Inc.)

compatibility 134

compiler 9

compile-time binding (see message binding)

compliance 203

completeness 112, 152, 156

completing projects 48, 88, 154

complexity 22, 82, 116, 150, 184, 186

components 25, 32, 206

composition 18, 24, 198

compound documents 23

computer-aided software engineering (CASE) 9, 38

concepts of OOD 31, 40

concrete class 25

configuration management 9

confusion 31

containment 19, 24

copying objects 192

costs

of development 90

of object-oriented development 34, 222

of testing and support 210

coupling 150, 204, 226, 228

Covey, Stephen 47

"creeping features" 86, 112

customers 26, 50, 64, 104, 124, 126, 237

customer support 203, 210

cutting size of development staff 32

D

dangling reference 196

data 7

data-oriented design 178

data member (see also member) 25

debugger 9

decisions 160

deep copy 192

derived class (see also subclass) 14, 25, 170, 172

design 26, 46, 78, 103, 106, 118, 148, 167

developers 4, 26, 35, 50, 56, 62, 74, 98, 124, 162, 236

development (see also software development) 26, 82

development time 21, 32, 80, 152

development tools 8, 32, 35, 42, 60, 131, 142, 237

dishonesty 94

distributed programs 44

Djikstra, Edsger 22

documentation 160

domain 25

Donovan, John 84

Duntemann, Jeff 7

dynamic binding (see message binding)

E

early binding (see message binding)

economics 134

education 31, 35, 41, 43, 46, 54, 142, 236

Eiffel 9, 46, 131, 140

embedded elements 44

Ellul, Jacques 66

encapsulation 11, 24, 114, 150, 172, 182

engineer 26

enlisting support 54, 58

enthusiasm 50, 58

enumeration 118

environment 131, 237

equality 194

event-driven systems 44

expectations 58, 100, 218, 237

experience 41, 43

F

FAQ on object-oriented development 250

factory method (see method)

faith 60

faster development (see development time)

features 64, 84, 86, 124, 234

feedback 75

forcing adoption of OOD 74

forgiveness 50

framework 25

Franklin, Benjamin 238

function member (see also member) 25

G

garbage collection 196

generality 112

goals 72

glossary of terms 24

Goldberg, Adele xi, xv, 3, 138, 238

graphical user interface (GUI) 32, 44

H

hardware 7

has-a relationship 19, 23, 168, 198

Holder, Wayne 2

holds-a relationship 19, 23

Hopper, Adm. Grace 54

hostility 54

Howitz, David 38

I

icons 44

identity 194

ignorance 110

implementation 12, 25, 47, 78, 114, 147, 156, 158

incomplete projects 48

inheritance 13, 24, 172

   implementation inheritance 14, 170

   interface inheritance 14, 16, 170

   multiple inheritance 14, 172

initialization 192

instance 12, 24

instance method (see method)

instance variable 25

instantiation 12

interface 11, 25, 114, 116, 150, 158, 182

   private 170

   protected 170

   public 170, 174

interface construction tools 9, 48

interpreter 9

invariants 150, 176

is-a relationship 14, 168, 170, 172

is-implemented-using relationship 168, 170

J

James I, King of England 71

K

Kahn, Douglas 138

Kahn, Philippe 138

Kennedy, Edward 72

Kidd, Jeff 97, 138

knows-about relationship 20

Krich, Dave 1

L

languages 9, 46, 60, 131

late binding (see message binding)

legacy applications 134

libraries 44

lightweight objects 198

Lily, Susan 138

linear development 82

Lorenz, Mark 97, 138

Love, Tom 140

lying 94

M

Machiavelli, Niccolo 53

manufacturers 136

mapping 22

management 71
(see also technical manager, upper management)
Marx, Karl 215
McCabe, Thomas J. 138
meeting deadlines 32
member 10, 25
data member 25
function member 25
member-by-member copy 192
memory leak 196, 198
message 10, 24, 44, 204
message binding 17
dynamic (late, run-time) binding 17
static (early, compile-time) binding 17
message dispatching 17
message proliferation 204
method 10, 25
class method 25
factory method 25
instance method 25
methodology 37, 44, 46, 60, 236
list of object-oriented methodologies 78
metrics 96
Meyers, Scott 139
Microsoft
OLE 2.0 21, 23, 131, 132, 136
Windows 131, 132, 137
milestone 26
mission-critical custom applications (MCCAs) 134
modularity 22, 32, 44
Mudd, Roger 72

N

new features (see features)
NeXT Computer, Inc. 1
NEXTSTEP 21, 131, 132

OpenStep 8, 131

O

object 9, 24, 167
assigning 192
copying 192
initializing 192
references 196
testing for equality 194
testing for identity 194
Objective-C 42, 114, 140
objectives 72
object-oriented methodology (see methodology)
Object Pascal 42
object technology 38
misuse of 162
OLE 2.0 (see Microsoft)
oozing objects 182
OpenDoc 23, 131
OpenStep (see NeXT Computer, Inc.)
operating system 8
optimism 2
orphaning objects 197
overriding 15
overselling 58
ownership 197

P

Pages by Pages 2
Pages Software Inc 1-3, 113
Paine, Thomas 167
Papaccio, Philip N. 83
paradigm 26, 126
ParcPlace Systems xv
pass-by-reference 198

pass-by-value 198

permission 54

perspective 60

politics 53, 134

polymorphism 16, 24, 200

poor reasons for going object-oriented 32

Pope, Alexander 31

presentation 44

pressure 76

principles of OOD 9, 42

problem domain 22, 110

problems in development 36

process-oriented design 178

productivity 98

program 8, 25

programming languages (see languages)

project 25

    pilot projects 35, 80, 237

    schedule 106, 234

    status 100, 152, 234

    successive releases 64

proliferation 198

promises 58, 154

protocols 16

prototype 26, 48, 88, 149

Q

quality assurance 203

R

read-only memory (ROM) 8

Reagan, Ronald 72

rearchitecting 82, 120, 122, 158

reference 196

reference counting 196

reinventing the wheel 160

religious fervor 60

resistance 56

reuse 21, 176, 215

    costs 222

    difficulty 216, 224, 226

    expectations 218

    focus on code reuse 220

    planning for 224, 229, 237

review 42

    code review 151, 234

    design review 151, 161, 209, 234

    feature review 234

    project review 41, 238

revision 78

rewriting (see also rearchitecting) 158

risk management 32, 57, 66, 92

ROM (read-only memory) 8

run-time binding (see message binding)

S

Santayana, George 233, 241

schedule 35, 80, 234, 235

self-deception 94

self-discipline 147

Shakespeare, William 203

shallow copy 192

simulations 10

skill 46, 98

slicing objects 192

Smalltalk 9, 46, 131, 140

Smith, Capt. Edward J. 103

software 8

software development (see also software engineering)— 7, 36, 233 software engineering 26

    neglect of 31, 32, 76

source code management (SCM) 9

specialization 14, 24

specifications 42, 84, 90, 234, 238

Spelhaug, Larry 127

Spencer, Henry 138

spiral development model 83, 236

stale reference 196

standards 150, 236

static binding (see message binding)

static type checking (see type checking)

Steinman, Jan xi

strong type checking (see type checking)

structured development 66, 108

subclass (see also derived class) 14, 25

subsystem 25, 156, 158

SunDog 2, 44

superclass (see also base class) 14, 25

Sutherland, Jeff 138

switch statements 200

T

Taligent, Inc. xi, 132, 139

    CommonPoint 8, 23, 131

technical manager 4, 26, 50, 71

technical support (see customer support)

technique 66

technology 134

testing 26, 32, 90, 203, 204, 206, 208, 237

terminology 24

tools (see development tools)

training (see education)

type checking 17, 24

    strong (static) type checking 17

    weak (dynamic) type checking 17

U

unrealistic expectations 50, 76

upper management 4, 26, 50, 54, 64

user interface 8, 9, 26

users (see customers)

utilities 8

V

visibility 204, 226

W

waterfall development cycle 82

Watson, Arthur H. 138

white-box testing 206

Whorf, Benjamin 131

Windows (see Microsoft)

workbenches 209

wrong reasons for going object-oriented 32